Before and after

SEPTEMBER 11, 2001

Before and after
SEPTEMBER 11, 2001
An Asian Perspective

Ateneo Center for Asian Studies

ATENEO CENTER FOR ASIAN STUDIES
School of Social Sciences
Loyola Schools
Third Floor, Social Sciences Building
Loyola Heights, Quezon City
P.O. Box 154, Manila 1099
Telephone: 4266001 loc. 5280

Book and cover design by Jim Imbong
Photograph by Brother Benjamin Abadiano

The publication of this volume has been made possible through the support of the Konrad Adenauer Center for Journalism at the Ateneo de Manila University.

The National Library of the Philippines CIP Data

Recommended entry:

Ateneo Center for Asian Studies.
Before and after September 11, 2001 : an Asian perspective. – Quezon City: ADMU, 2004
1 v

1. Terrorism – Asia. 2. Terrorism – United States. 3. Foreign policy – U.S. 4. Ethnic Conflict – Asia. I. Title.

HV6432 363.32'095 2004 P041000527
ISBN 971-92296-4-0

Table of Contents

Acknowledgments

One year after the terrorist tragedy in America, the Ateneo Center for Asian Studies sponsored a conference entitled "Terrorism, Peace, and Development in Asia after September 11, 2001." This book is a collection of the papers that were presented at the conference.

The conference was held in cooperation with the Ateneo Center for Social Policy and Public Affairs and the Ateneo Graduate School of Business, and was made possible with the support of the Konrad Adenauer Stiftung.

Credit is due Benjamin T. Tolosa Jr., Ph.D., chair of the Department of Political Science, Ateneo de Manila University, for editing all the papers.

Special thanks to Bro. Ben of ILAWAN for the wonderful image used for the cover of this book.

Contributors

Jose S. Arcilla, S.J.
Professor, Department of History, Ateneo de Manila University

Aileen S.P. Baviera
Associate Professor, and Dean of the Asian Center, University of the Philippines

Cielito F. Habito
Professor, Department of Economics, Ateneo de Manila University. Former Director-General, National Economic and Development Authority (NEDA)

Benito O. Lim
Lecturer, Department of Political Science, Ateneo de Manila University

Ellen H. Palanca
Professor, Department of Economics and Director, Ateneo Center for Asian Studies and the Chinese Studies Program

Angelo T. Reyes
Secretary of National Defense, Republic of the Philippines

Julkipli M. Wadi
Assistant Professor, Institute of Islamic Studies, University of the Philippines

Foreword

Anna Miren Gonzalez-Intal, Ph.D.

September 11, 2001, was the day the world changed in some very important ways. It showed that the evil of terrorism had reached a new level of mercilessness and devastation. Although terrorism had been a serious concern in some parts of the developing world, the September 11 terror attack on two key symbols of Western capitalism and political power also brought to the fore the chilling fact that terrorists could hit anywhere. It highlighted the stark reality that although the Cold War might have ended, the world was now faced with a different kind of war, one no less daunting, and perhaps even more difficult. It shattered the myth of invulnerability of the U.S. mainland. It made the threat of the use of biological and chemical weapons for terrorism even more real and serious.

September 11, 2001, reshaped the United States' foreign policy priorities. Specifically, it led the United States to view its bilateral foreign relations primarily from the perspective of security and anti-terrorism. At the same time, it underscored the importance of cooperation and common resolve among countries of differing persuasions to address the problem of international terrorism. It also made the rest of the world see the immediacy and preeminence of economic and political reform to counter fundamentalism and extremism as responses to the injustices and miserable reality that so many live under. Some countries restricted certain "freedoms" in the interest of national and personal safety. It hurt international trade and investments substantially and contributed to the deepening of the recessionary processes in 2001.

September 11, 2001, highlighted the importance to world security of ensuring peace and stability not only in the Middle East but also in Central Asia. It brought an end to the Taliban rule in Afghanistan. It made the United States not balk at the use of military power as demonstrated by the U.S.-led war against Saddam Hussein. In Southeast Asia it has brought great awareness of the region's strong links with the terrorist networks of the Middle East and Central Asia and the vulnerability of the ASEAN countries as launching pads and targets for attack. In our own country, it brought U.S.-supported anti-terrorism initiatives that led nationalists to the streets to protest U.S. interference in sovereign affairs.

On the first anniversary of that fateful day in September, it was indeed fitting that the Ateneo Center for Asian Studies of the Ateneo Loyola Schools, in cooperation with the Ateneo Center for Social Policy and Public Affairs, and the Ateneo Graduate School of Business, and with the support of the Konrad Adenauer Stiftung, sponsored the conference on "Terrorism, Peace and Development in Asia after September 11, 2001." I would like to congratulate the Ateneo Center for Asian Studies and its Director, Dr. Ellen H. Palanca, for spearheading the conference and for putting together this volume of the papers presented at the conference so that a wider audience may have access to them. The book makes an important contribution as the papers provide us with a broader and deeper understanding, especially from the Asian perspective, of the nexus of poverty, justice, religion, politics, power, development, terrorism, and peace that have been at the forefront of global history and consciousness especially since September 11, 2001.

Introduction

Ellen H. Palanca, Ph.D.

On September 11, 2002, one year after the 9/11 tragedy, the Ateneo Center for Asian Studies sponsored a conference on "Terrorism, Peace, and Development in Asia after September 11, 2001." This book is a collection of the papers presented during the conference.

The 9/11 terrorist attacks have changed the world completely. The impact on the Middle East was evident in the year after the attacks. The conflict between India and Pakistan escalated almost immediately after the events. Several events and developments in Asia prior to 9/11 have been in retrospect linked to the activities of both regional and global terrorism. Regional terrorist groups have been found to be connected to or part of global terrorist networks. In the year after 9/11, several Southeast Asian countries, namely the Philippines, Malaysia, and Singapore, arrested Islamic extremists allegedly linked to al-Qaeda. The strong resolve of the U.S. to fight terrorism changed, or gave its government the excuse to change, its foreign policy and relations with countries all over the world. The imminent question then was whether Southeast Asia would become the next front of the U.S. war on terrorism. This was coming on the heels of the "liberation" of Afghanistan from the Taliban, as well as the likelihood of war in Iraq.

The 9/11 terrorist acts were attacks of Muslim radical extremists against the United States. Prof. Julkipli Wadi's paper, "Ambivalence, Ferment, and Trade-Off Since 9/11," traces the underlying causes and conditions that led to the apparently incomprehensible acts of 9/11, and analyzes their ramifications in Southeast Asia. The feeling of ambivalence among the Muslims stems from their disapproval of the radical terrorist Muslims as well as their strong resentment of the American "double standard" foreign policy in the Middle East. The 9/11 attacks also brought about heightened ferment among Muslims against U.S. hegemony, which emerged at the end of the Cold War as pan-Islamic groups among them found more opportunities to politicize Islam.

Finally, Wadi discusses the changes that are happening in Southeast Asian Islamic countries after 9/11. Malaysia and Indonesia are predominantly Muslim countries, while in the Philippines the Muslims are in the minority. Unlike the India-Pakistan and Israel-Palestine disputes, the conflicts in these countries do not involve territorial issues based on religion or ideology. Their internal political conflicts, however, are due to the emergence of Muslim fundamentalists and militants, as well as their close links to the structure of global political Islam. (The bombing of Bali in October 2002 demonstrated this.)

While the post-Cold War unipolar power configuration has intensified the position of radical Muslims, 9/11 has reshuffled the global configuration of powers. To investigate this new power configuration, Prof. Aileen Baviera explores the relations of the United States with the international community, in general, and the major Asian powers—China, Japan, India, and Russia—in particular, after the 9/11 incidents. Her essay also criticizes the U.S. for what she deems as its unilateral and arrogant foreign policy, even as it sought to lead the campaign against terrorism and get UN approval for its war against Iraq. The message of such a policy, she feels, "is that in the so-called war against terror, the use of force is legitimate, sovereign, and human rights are of no consequence, international cooperation is desirable but not necessary, and might makes right."

Although the nations that constitute the ASEAN group welcomed the United States' fight against terrorism, the extent of cooperation of the various member countries was contingent on political and economic concessions given to them. Indonesia received an economic package and made concessions for a loosening of the human rights watch on its military. Nevertheless, the government's posture towards the U.S. campaign against terrorism was rather ambivalent as it did not want to displease the politically strong fundamentalist group in the country. Mahathir of Malaysia, on the other hand, gained substantial political mileage with the now-justified force of quelling the power of its fundamentalist Muslims.

The Philippines, meantime, was one of the first countries to pledge support to the U.S.-led campaign against terrorism, much to the chagrin of nationalists and peace advocates among its politicians and citizens. While the majority welcomed the renewal of military ties with the U.S. due to their fear of the growing Abu Sayyaf problem, a sizeable minority opposed such a government policy. Those who did so cited the issue of sovereignty, which would suffer from U.S. military presence in the country, and argued that aligning with the U.S. could make the Philippines more of a target for terrorist attacks. Moreover, some felt that the peace process, both with the National Democratic Front (NDF) and Moro Islamic Liberation Front (MILF), would be jeopardized since any protest or expression of dissatisfaction by these groups would very likely put them in the category of terrorist groups.

The justification given by the Philippine government with regard to its policy to support the U.S. war against terrorism and allow R.P.-U.S. joint military exercises is presented in the essay by then Sec. of National Defense Angelo T. Reyes. He explains that the Philippines-U.S. joint military exercises (Balikatan), which had ceased to be practiced since the pullout of the U.S. military bases, were necessary to fight the growing terrorist acts of the Abu Sayyaf, who were linked to al-Qaeda. There was also assurance that the military exercises were to be conducted within the bounds of the Constitution, i.e., the U.S. military would not be involved in combat but only in training activities, and that there would be no permanent basing and support facility built. Perhaps the most important justification was the much-needed upgrading of the AFP which was the expected outcome from the U.S.$92.3 million fund support and training provided by the U.S. government.

Based essentially on Church history, the article by Rev. Jose S. Arcilla, S.J., gives a review of political conflict seemingly rooted in religious differences. It recounts cases dating from as early as the period of the Roman Empire, which persecuted the Jews as well as the Christians; religious wars during the Medieval era between Christians; as well as the conflicts that arose when Christianity was brought to Asia. In the Philippines, the spread of Christianity, which replaced the indigenous cults and religions, was both the reason for as well as a means of maintaining the Spanish process of colonization. Arcilla conjectures that "conflicts occur only when society has reached a certain level of political and cultural sophistication." He goes on to propose the theory that the reason the Spaniards were not able to subjugate the Muslims in Maguindanao and Sulu was because they were relatively sophisticated politically.

Prof. Benito Lim's essay discusses the fifty-five-year India-Pakistan War, which represents another political conflict that on the surface is based on religious difference (Hindus vs. Muslims). It attributes a host of factors to the protracted conflict, which at times has involved state terrorism. While the British colonial divide-and-rule legacy had been used to explain the conflict, it can in fact be traced to centuries before the British rule when communal skirmishes periodically arose among diverse religious sects and cultures.

Relating the India-Pakistan War to the 9/11 events, Professor Lim discusses how the conflict is connected to Afghanistan and the personage who is largely acknowledged to be the protagonist of 9/11, Osama bin Laden. Dissatisfied with the Indian rule of Kashmir, many young Kashmiris went to Afghanistan and Pakistan for CIA-funded training in guerrilla warfare. Some went back to Kashmir to fight for its liberation in 1991, but many joined the international Muslim group, led by Osama bin Laden, that went to Afghanistan to fight against the Russians. This international group also attracted Muslims from other countries, such as Indonesia, Malaysia, Chechnya, the Philippines, and China, to go to Afghanistan and Pakistan for training. Osama bin Laden became a "household name to young and idealistic Muslim jihadis."

The last essay in this collection by Dr. Cielito Habito presents the effects of the 9/11 attacks on Asian economies. The fear of similar attacks on planes has significantly affected the international tourism sector. In Asia, this was clear from the statistics showing the reduced number of flights of many airlines as well as plummeting hotel occupancy rates. The effect on the insurance sector was directly borne by the insurance companies in the U.S. and Europe. The consequence on all has been higher insurance cost, which is being transferred to consumers in the form of higher airfares with the addition of a surcharge to cover increased insurance cost; it has also affected the prices of traded goods, to reflect higher freight insurance cost. The decline in the U.S. economy after 9/11 has negatively affected exports of many Asian countries, for which the U.S. is an important market.

Despite the economic concessions made by the U.S. to some countries in Asia—Pakistan, the Philippines, and to a lesser extent, Indonesia—for their support of its campaign against terrorism, one sees that the ultimate result of terrorism and the so-called war against terror in economic terms has been negative. Pakistan's economy suffered severe setbacks in its tourism and exports, while the economies of the Philippines and Indonesia have remained in the doldrums due to the political instability created by the threat of terrorism. On the other hand, those of Korea and the other Southeast Asian countries that did not face much threat from terrorism in the first place were able to recover. Dr. Habito concludes that "(the) lack of peace and security in communities and in society as a whole, and of general political stability provide an inhospitable environment for economic activities, whether for big business or for small and medium enterprises (SMEs)."

Since the first anniversary of the 9/11 attacks, many events have continued to threaten the peace and well-being of nations and communities all over the world. Aside from the war on Iraq which started in February 2003 and continues to drag on (as of publication date), many more terrorist attacks (among them, the bombings in Bali and Davao, recently in Istanbul, and incessantly in the Middle East) have taken place and continue to take place. To this day, for developed and developing countries, peace and amelioration of life remain as elusive as ever.

Although peace and development as issues have not been thoroughly tackled in this volume, the essays here delve into the historical, political, and social roots of the 9/11 attacks and their implications on the economy and on society as a whole. One notes that the issues raised and analyses made by the eminent scholars in these articles continue to be relevant and useful, and in fact may provide a basis for understanding developments that are yet to unfold.

Ambivalence, Ferment, and Trade-off Since 9/11

Julkipli M. Wadi

The attacks in New York and Washington on September 11, 2001 caused unprecedented shock waves in many parts of the world. It radically transformed the context of world affairs, changed the rules of the game of international politics, and shaped anew the regional security condition in many countries. Consequently, 9/11 both heightened and diminished old fault lines of world tensions but created new ones. New alliances were formed and new enemies were identified even as foes became friends, and friends became foes. More particularly, the United States found new justification in broadening its power and influence in many parts of the world as war on international terrorism ramified into regime change. What is the general sentiment in the Muslim world on 9/11? Why is it characterized by ambivalence? How can such ambivalence be explained in the context of ferment in the Muslim world?

This short essay posits that the ambivalence of Muslim society toward 9/11 is due to the contradictory engagement by the United States in the Middle East and other regions. While the United States has gained international support from a number of countries, at least, on regional and state levels, such support, however, does not sit well among the Muslim masses. This ambivalence is not only a cause of anxiety for the United States and its allies but for Muslim governments as well: 9/11 crystallized the looming tension in the Muslim world which has remained since the beginnings of Pax

Americana in the nineteenth century. The ambivalence many Muslims today harbor toward the United States is the product of a new conflict configuration in the Islamic world ushered in by American hegemony particularly in the Middle East. This tension is reinforced by unwavering U.S. support for Israel despite its oppressive policy against the Palestinians.

9/11 and U.S. Foreign Policy

It is observed that the government of the United States is consistent in delinking 9/11 and U.S. foreign policy in the face of growing resentment from Muslims worldwide. Despite the barbarity of the attacks on Washington and New York, a considerable number of Muslims believe that 9/11 was triggered by U.S. foreign policy particularly in the Middle East. In the Gallup poll of nine Muslim countries with 9,924 respondents, conducted between December 2001 and January 2002 and released in February 2002, the ambivalence is seen when "67 percent saw the September 11 attacks as morally unjustified, while 15 percent of the respondents said they were morally justified." Moreover, "77 percent said the U.S. military action in Afghanistan was morally unjustified, compared with 9 percent who said it was morally justified." Despite overwhelming evidence unearthed by the United States against those who perpetrated the attack, 61 percent of Muslim respondents "did not believe Arab groups carried out the September 11 terrorist attacks." Moreover, "58 percent of those surveyed had unfavorable opinions, compared with 11 percent who had favorable views." The poll respondents also believed that "the United States was aggressive and biased against Islamic values" especially "against Palestinians." Finally, the poll underscored the fact that the residents of nine Muslim countries called the United States "ruthless and arrogant" while most of them are "resentful of the superpower."[1]

It is clear that while the United States would like to delink 9/11 and its foreign policy particularly in the Muslim world and convince Arab/Muslim states of such position, the views expressed by

1 CNN.com—Poll: Muslims call U.S. "ruthless, arrogant"—26 February 2002. The countries included in the survey are Pakistan, Iran, Indonesia, Turkey, Lebanon, Morocco, Kuwait, Jordan, and Saudi Arabia.

the Muslim masses reveal otherwise. Ironically, while this view may be understandable in the Muslim world, the survey on Americans and Europeans by the Chicago Council of Foreign Relations and the German Marshall Fund of the United States last September 4, 2002 reflect the views of many Muslims. Of nine thousand Europeans and Americans surveyed, "55 percent of Europeans believe the attacks by the radical al-Qaeda Islamist group on the World Trade Center and the Pentagon were a product of U.S. policy overseas to some degree." The poll also revealed that "many Europeans as well as Americans are critical of Pres. George W. Bush's handling of foreign policy issue" (*PDI,* Sept. 5, 2002, 9, c. 3).

The findings of the two highly respected polling institutions would have been easily dismissed by the White House as they do not reflect the foreign policy pursued by Pres. George Bush. However, the position of the Muslim masses is seconded by no less than the Central Intelligence Agency (CIA) which has said "that the U.S. counterterrorist operations around the world may not eliminate the threat of future attacks because they fail to address the root causes of terrorism." The CIA is unequivocal in identifying the "root cause" to include the "continued instability in Afghanistan, challenges facing Saudi rulers and the festering Israeli-Palestinian conflict." The CIA also accepts that these issues are "likely to fuel radicalism in the Muslim world." It is clear that unless U.S. foreign policy in the Muslim world particularly the Middle East is restructured by addressing the "root cause" of the problem, which revolves around the Arab-Israeli conflict, one has no difficulty in agreeing with the CIA that "the underlying causes that drive terrorists will persist" (*PDI,* Oct. 30, 2002, 14, c. 1).

Do the polls, including the report of the CIA, mean that most Muslims support al-Qaeda of Osama bin Laden? Not necessarily. What is certain is while the majority of Muslims may not support the radical al-Qaeda, they loathe, however, the "double standard" of U.S. foreign policy in the Middle East, especially America's continuing support for Israel despite its atrocities against Palestinians. It must be remembered that the continuing illegal occupation by Israel of the Palestinian homeland is shared by many Muslims as the major "root cause" of the problem and constitutes the main raison d'être for the radicalization of Islamic movements in the Middle East.[2] Hence, while majority of Muslims may not agree with the perpetrators behind 9/11, they equally condemn the unmitigated U.S. support for Israel and the state terror unleashed against Palestinians.

Underscoring the Ferment in the Muslim World

The current ferment that engulfs the world today, as shown by the attacks on September 11, is the product of accumulating tensions in the Muslim world. The tension is brought about by the confluence of both international and domestic problems—imposed and otherwise—reinforced by the geopolitical and strategic interests of the big powers in the Middle East. It is further enflamed by the collapse of the erstwhile Soviet Union that was formally sealed with the end of the Cold War. Since then, the international order was swayed under a unipolar system making the United States dominant in world politics with no major power—not even the United Nations and the Security Council—capable of balancing America's global hegemony. As a consequence, the character of the international system changed considerably in the post-Cold War period while ethnic conflict, religious and political activism, and transnational crime in many parts of the world arose unhindered. The *ummah* (community that adheres to an Islamic way of life) has not been left untouched by these developments.

Today, the Muslim world represents a mixture of contrasting realities. It has a population of more than 1.2 billion, the largest among world religions with two-thirds as Muslim majorities under Arab/Muslim regimes and one-third as minorities under non-Muslim governments. Yet, a range of structural, economic, political, cultural, and religious contradictions plagues many parts of the Muslim world. Undeniably, while the Muslim world is blessed with rich human and natural resources and occupies strategic areas and regions, most of today's major conflicts involve Muslim countries and minorities.

2 According to Osama bin Laden, apart from other forms of control and domination by the United States in the Muslim world, Israeli aggression and illegal occupation of Palestinian lands and the support of the United States for Israel are the major causes in his waging of jihad against America. See, for instance, Peter L. Bergen 2001, *Holy War Inc.: Inside the Secret World of Osama bin Laden* (New York: The Free Press). See also Bernard Lewis 1998, "License to Kill," *Foreign Affairs* (November/December).

To say the least, there are no Muslim countries today in complete harmony with each other. Moreover, while the Muslim world has billionaires, kings, princes, and thousands of rich and famous, most of the Muslim countries and minorities belong to the Third World with poverty and unemployment rising in enormous proportions.

In spite of Islam's vision of equality, just government, and Islamic development, many Muslim countries and minorities continue to struggle with a feudal structure in their political system ranging from monarchy, dictatorship, authoritarianism, and "illiberal" democracy. While Saudi Arabia, for instance, ranked 68th in development out of 162 countries in 1999, its immediate neighbor, Yemen, ranked 133rd. Amid their vision for global ummah, the Sunni-Shia schism continues to delay the effort of much stronger Islamic rapprochement, cooperation, and unity. Finally, despite the promise of the Organization of the Islamic Conference (OIC), the same organization is torn between the vision of Islamic solidarity and the principle of national sovereignty. This is why the OIC has not played a significant role in many critical issues facing the Muslim world at present.

The social contradiction was sharpened in the Middle East when colonial powers strengthened control and access over the strategic resources of the region, particularly oil. This issue of control and access to strategic resources is linked to the need of the United States to have a strong ally (e.g., Israel) to serve not only as a buffer state but as a hegemonic partner in the region. This is why despite the numerous resolutions in the UN supporting the Middle East peace process and the right of the Palestinian people to self-determination, the United States has consistently sided with Israel and blatantly disregarded pertinent UN resolutions.

Apart from Israel, the United States pampered moderate Arab monarchies and governments, e.g., Saudi Arabia, Kuwait, Egypt, while subjecting the so-called rogue states (e.g., Iraq, Iran, Syria, Libya) to tremendous pressure and economic sanctions. The double-standard policy of the United States crystallized when it allegedly brought democracy to Kuwait during the 1991 Gulf War. Yet it did not raise a finger to halt the unmitigated expansion of Israel in the West Bank, the Gaza Strip, and other Palestinian areas. Instead, the United States encouraged an arms race in the region and strengthened its military alliance with Saudi Arabia, Kuwait, and Turkey. Thus the United States rode on internal tensions in the region to create a hegemonic zone with Israel and moderate Arab regimes serving under the behest of America.

Moreover, the form of conflicts in the Muslim world began changing from inter-state war to conflicts perpetrated by nonstate actors, the so-called irregular warriors, or postmodern terrorists (Tibi 1998, 214). Subsequently, it widened the cleavage among major forces, classes, and groupings in the region even as claim and counterclaim for legitimacy ensued. Meanwhile, the interpretation of Islamic teaching and doctrine became polarized, making Islam a serious subject of deconstruction and counterconstruction. This problem is heightened at a time whenIslam has been pictured as having two major faces during the past few decades: Islam according to the state and Islam according to Islamic movements, i.e., political Islam (Ayoob 1981, 272). This political bivalence in Islam can be seen as "normal" since it reflects the age-old tensions in the Muslim world since the seventh century onward (e.g., the Ali-Muawiyyah dispute, Sunni-Shia schism, Umayyad-Abbasid rivalry, Arab nationalism-pan-Islamic dialectic). Specifically, intra-Arab/Muslim conflict is inherent particularly in the Middle East. However, conflict turns globally problematic when the politics in the region gets linked to the economic and geopolitical interests of big powers like the United States.

In the post-Cold War era, the absence of a countervailing force to balance United States hegemony has emboldened many Islamic movements worldwide. First, it allows them to fill in the power vacuum among opposition groups in the Muslim world and gives them the opportunity to forge a massive network worldwide. Second, it broadens their concern beyond the purview of their respective ethnic interests and nationalities and paves the way for constructing Islam as a political ideology to combat what they saw as Western hegemony, international Zionism, and Arab/Muslim puppetry. These characterize al-Qaeda under the leadership of Osama bin Laden.

The politicization and subsequent transnationalization of Islam is a product of a long-standing rivalry between Arab nationalism and pan-Islamism since the early 1900s. The failure of the former to use Islam as the basis of a political system and as a framework of development in the Arab world has provided opportunities for pan-Islamic groups to claim support and legitimacy from marginal sectors of Muslim society. It is reinforced by the failure of Arab nationalism to get rid of neocolonial vestiges in the Middle East and other parts of the Muslim world. The sway of Islamic movements has increased with the eclipse of reform movements in Muslim-dominated areas and secessionist groups in non-Muslim dominated areas.

Since the Afghan War in the 1980s, these two kinds of struggles have forged strong linkages with each other. It thus appears that the neo-Islamic struggle is global— making their target not only their immediate enemies, e.g., Arab/Muslim- and Christian-dominated governments, but also the very source of global hegemony (e.g., America) and all that it symbolizes (e.g., capitalism, power). Taking their cue from the uselessness of petty acts of violence in their respective locales, Islamic movements have heightened their struggle by attacking the heartland of America—as shown in the September 11 attacks. What the perpetrators of 9/11 needed was will and capability. Ironically, they simply had to use U.S. technology to destroy the very symbols of America's economic and political power.

Impact and Trade-off in Southeast Asia

The impact of 9/11 is far-reaching in Southeast Asia given the relatively a similar feeling of ambivalence common among many Muslims in the region. While they do not support the horrible attacks in New York and Washington, many of them despise the double-standard policies of the United States in the Middle East, particularly its inconsistent stance towards the Palestinian problem. Undeniably, the United States scored well in forging ties with the Association of Southeast Asian Nations (ASEAN) as a regional partner in combating terrorism and successfully eliciting support from individual countries, though in varying degrees and using different arrangements. It was shown in the arrest of suspected members of Jamaah Islamiyyah, Laskar Jihad, Abu Sayyaf, who are alleged to be connected with al-Qaeda. However, before ASEAN extended cooperation, the United States had to offer juicy political and economic concessions to individual member-countries. As Indonesia was projected as being the "weakest link" in the U.S. war on international terrorism in Southeast Asia, the United States had to ease up its human rights monitoring on Indonesia and had to accelerate the extension of an economic package as well. This shift of policy does not only strengthen Indonesia's political and military position against ethnic, nationalist, and liberation movements in many parts of the country, it also provides much needed respite after being isolated by the international community since the independence struggle in East Timor. Despite Prime Minister Mahathir Mohammed's critical posturing vis-à-vis U.S. foreign policy for the past few years, the war on international terrorism provided Malaysia a new ally that would not only strengthen Malaysia's standing as an emerging economic tiger. The new bilateral agreement between Malaysia and the United States also strengthens Malaysia's policy of quelling internal dissent and resolving territorial disputes in its favor, including possibly the Sabah claim. The implementation of stricter immigration laws and the massive deportation of Indonesians and Filipinos (mostly Muslims) to the southern Philippines was just one of Malaysia's domestic and regional policies.

In the Philippines, while the government had been fighting the Abu Sayyaf for some time, it was precisely the threat from the Abu Sayyaf that convinced the United States to provide much needed economic and military assistance. It must be remembered that the Philippines has been out of the radar screen of U.S. foreign policy since the closing of the U.S. bases in the Philippines in the early 1990s. Subsequently, despite the hazy evidence linking the Abu Sayyaf to al-Qaeda, the campaign against the Abu Sayyaf proved advantageous to the Armed Forces of the Philippines (AFP) as it revived military and technical ties from the United States. Moreover, the war on international terrorism emboldens the government to take a hardline stance against Muslim secessionist movements and Philippine Communists by using the renewed relationship as a bargaining chip against insurgent groups. With the New People's Army tagged as terrorist organization, the framing of a comprehensive peace policy will have to take a back seat since the government will not be pressured to craft one. The same can be asserted against the Moro

Islamic Liberation Front and other Moro fronts in Mindanao. The Philippine government must be sending this strong message: "If you do not keep quiet we'll call you terrorists. By that time, you won't be fighting the AFP, you'll be fighting the United States."

Trends and Implications

The war against international terrorism in Southeast Asia is certainly faced with both old and new problems. For the past few years, there has been a looming politicization of Islam by significant quarters of the Muslim community in the region that has coincided with the struggle for decolonization, reform, and self-determination in Asia. Some of them antedated the Cold War, others originated during the height of Pax Americana, while the rest remained and continue to metamorphose. As the United States internationalizes the war against terrorism, many of these struggles are alluded to as having the same genus of terrorism catapulting the problem into an admixture of issues that border on semantics and history.

In the past, the threat posed by militant Islamic movements in Southeast Asia was embryonic and transitory and mostly geared towards either reform or self-determination within the limited boundaries of states in the region. It was far from becoming a security threat on a regionwide scale much less one capable of changing the political landscape of Southeast Asia. Indeed, their capability to inflict damage has been substantially enhanced in the last few years but their linkage with al-Qaeda was momentary and their network links with other militant Islamic groups in the region remained hazy. There was no unified source of dissent in Southeast Asia that could galvanize them together. The role of Osama bin Laden and the training and experience they got in Afghanistan had certainly given the Islamic movements greater impetus worldwide. But for the intensity of their cause to remain and to continue, it had to be sustained by contentious local and regional issues that they could consistently rally around. While it is true that Islam could serve as a source of ideology and a potent force for political dissent, it was, however constrained within the Southeast Asian culture of balance and moderation. Moreover, Islam was interpreted in varying ways by different Islamic movements and personalities in the countries of the region.

Finally, Southeast Asia does not have Jerusalem or Kashmir that can be a cause of pressing rival claims between and among countries and political groups. For instance, while the Sabah and Spratlys issues have been a cause of tensions for the past few years, these two issues have remained untainted with religion and ideology.

Recently, however, political Islam in Southeast Asia has changed substantially. It has grown with the rapid flow of communication and transportation and the influx of transnational Islamic movements from the Middle East and South Asia. Hence, the originally segmented and limited areas of influence of politicized Muslim groups in the area are emboldened (real or otherwise) thus giving the appearance of a major Islamic upheaval in Southeast Asia with a regionwide support structure of global political Islam in the area. This point was vividly shown in the Bali bombing that rocked Indonesia on October 12, 2002. It killed nearly 200 foreigners, mostly Australians. It was, so far, the most horrible attack in Southeast Asia since 9/11. The incident came as a surprise because Islamic movements in Southeast Asia are very much different from those in the Middle East, with their causes diverse and their political ideology and linkages only nascent. While Indonesia, the Philippines, and other countries in the region had been racked by bombings by a host of Muslim extremist groups in the past, the destruction, sophistication, and message of the Bali bombing were qualitatively different. At any rate, the problem must be fully understood in the context of issues in the region. Violence and terror cannot just undermine overnight the inherent character of Southeast Asian Islam that has been imbued for centuries by a unique form of spirituality, religious tolerance, and cultural harmony.

References

Ayoob, Mohammed. 1981. *The Politics of Islamic Reassertion.* London: Croom Helm Ltd.

Bergen, Peter. 2001. *Holy War Inc.: Inside the Secret World of Osama bin Laden.* New York: The Free Press.

Tibi, Bassam. 1998. *Conflict and War in the Middle East: From Interstate War to the Challenge of Islamic Fundamentalism.* 2d ed. London: MacMillan Press, Ltd.

Lewis, Bernard. 1998. "License to Kill." *Foreign Affairs* (November/December).

CNN.com—Poll: Muslims Call U.S. "Ruthless, Arrogant," February 26, 2002.

"Poll: US Foreign Policy Partly to Blame for 9/11." *Philippine Daily Inquirer*, September 5, 2002.

"CIA Doubts US Ability to Clear Threat of Future Attacks." *Philippine Daily Inquirer*, October 30, 2002.

International Terrorism, U.S. Foreign Policy and Great Power Relations in the Asia Pacific

Aileen S.P. Baviera

Since the end of the Cold War, the United States has been the single most powerful state in the world—from a comprehensive definition of power which is inclusive of military might (hard power), economic strength, advanced science and technology, rich human resources, and cultural as well as ideological influence (soft power).[1] The implosion of the Soviet Union and its breaking up relegated its successor states—Russia and the Commonwealth of Independent States (CIS)—to the role of third-rate players in global affairs. Europe, despite advances in community building and the absence of major threats, has remained reliant on the United States for its security and been unable to craft an independent vision that would help Europeans enjoy the hard-earned dividends of peace between East and West. Japan's economy has been mired in recession for a decade, weakening its claim to even a regional leadership and stifling moves to inch away from its relations with Washington. It is China that is the emerging new power—especially from the economic perspective—and it is increasingly assertive in its foreign policy.

1 The U.S. is expected to spend more on defense in 2003 than the next 15–20 biggest spenders combined. Its economy is more than twice as large as the next biggest economy—Japan. Spending on R&D nearly equaled those of the next seven richest countries combined. For a detailed discussion, see Stephen G. Brooks and William C. Wolfforth, "American Primacy in Perspective," *Foreign Affairs* (July–August 2002).

In terms of military strength and technological capacity, however, it remains many decades behind Washington.

Hegemony in a Posthegemonic World

There simply is no contesting the fact that the United States is, in relative as well as absolute terms, stronger than any country has ever been in the history of the modern world. It is also very much committed to the status quo, happy to exercise its leadership as the world's only superpower, although leadership over what and in what forms such leadership could be exercised in the post-Cold War period are questions that beg to be addressed.

In the immediate aftermath of the end of the Cold War, free markets, capitalists, and liberal democratic governments emerged the victors. But the triumph of capitalism and liberal democracy was obviously not enough to guarantee world peace or development, so the euphoria of the triumphalists did not last long. Nor was the argument of Fukuyama that at least part of the international community had already reached "the end of history" found convincing.[2] Ideological conflict was indeed no longer perceived as the threat to humanity that it had once been made out to be, but soon enough, wars and conflicts erupted anew that grew from humanity's even more primordial instincts—the desire for territory, the craving for ethnic and cultural identity, the contest for resources of the earth and its oceans, among others.

At the same time, new issues and fault lines emerged. The inevitable backlash against globalization came, even as countries—or at least their governments and elites—moved closer towards integration. Integration is taking place through the international trading regimes, through the discipline imposed by international financial institutions, through advances in telecommunications, including cable TV and the Internet, and through the dominating discourses on structural adjustment, free trade, human rights, and good governance, among others. The backlash against globalization occurred in rural communities, in struggling enterprises, among indigenous

2 Francis Fukuyama argued that following the end of the Cold War, the victory of liberal democracy over Marxism-Lenism will lead to a new international accord where wars would be less likely to occur.

cultures, within fundamentalist religions, and from nationalist movements of the developing countries, but no less so than in factories, trade unions, among intellectuals and civil society organizations of the developed world.

Transnationalism became a phenomenon emblematic of the global village, with the unfortunate downside seen in transnational crime, including weapons proliferation, piracy, illegal trafficking in people and drugs, money laundering and other white-collar crimes, and international terrorism. New challenges to human security also emerged in the form of infectious diseases like AIDS and cross-border pollution, even while poverty remained widespread in many parts of the globe.

The so-called nontraditional challenges, which emerged, were obviously not so easy to address using U.S. military might, nor its technological superiority, nor its economic wealth. Nor could they be addressed without relying on the significant contributions of other governments, of international organizations, and, in many cases, even of NGOs. Solutions depended on the ability of the players to share information, to coordinate actions, to standardize policies, and take cooperative action while at the same time remaining sensitive to the still extant principle of state sovereignty and to cultural differences. The situation was, therefore, one where U.S. leadership was for the first time uncontested by any other major power—giving it the status of world hegemon,[3] but also one where U.S. leadership alone would be inadequate or even inappropriate for many of the new problems at hand.

Yet to the surprise and disappointment of many, including in the United States itself, the world's sole superpower would once more cave in to its impulse of going it alone. Under the current Bush administration, the U.S. is trying to remain the world's hegemon, despite the post-Cold War posthegemonic condition that prevails today. Moreover, it prefers to tread the path of unilateralism in a world that had essentially become multipolar. The current leaders in Washing-

3 In political science and international relations theory, Keohane and Nye define hegemony as the situation "when one state is powerful enough to maintain the essential rules governing inter-state relations, and willing to do so" (Robert O. Keohane and Joseph S. Nye Jr. , *Power and Interdependence: World Politics in Transition* [Boston: Little, Brown, 1977], 44.

ton have effectively reversed the previous Clinton administration's internationalist and multilateralist foreign policy thrusts.

The world could only watch while the U.S. trashed the Kyoto Protocol, which the international community had spent ten years negotiating. This was despite the fact that the U.S. is responsible for much of the polluting emissions that hasten global warming. It refused to place itself under the jurisdiction of the International Criminal Court, even threatening to withdraw its funding contributions for UN peacekeeping should others insist. It single-handedly scuttled the ABM Treaty with Russia, without so much as an acknowledgment of the impact on other parties concerned. Its entire attitude towards the United Nations is dismissive, often seeking UN support for its actions only as an afterthought and only to increase the legitimacy of otherwise unpalatable unilateral policies. Even its closest allies such as the members of NATO, Japan, and South Korea are not so much consulted as they are called upon to help enforce U.S. decisions, increasingly causing resentment and gradually degrading the quality of support to one that is offered only grudgingly.

Many in Washington appear to argue that the United States should maintain its role of a global policeman, a unique responsibility that requires that there should be no dilution of U.S. power and influence, even by the United Nations. After all, not all vestiges of the Cold War had disappeared. In the Asia Pacific region, the situation on the Korean peninsula remains fraught with the twin dangers of war and regime collapse. China and Taiwan continue to bicker over reunification or independence, with Beijing occasionally conducting missile-firing exercises across the Taiwan Straits on the one hand, and Taiwan purchasing more and better war equipment from the U.S. on the other. The modernization of China's military worries its smaller neighbors, particularly those embroiled in the territorial and jurisdictional disputes in the South China Sea. The India-Pakistan dispute over Kashmir flared anew, this time with a possible nuclear dimension following successful weapons tests by both sides. This, to the United States, was familiar ground, where familiar instruments of its hard power such as forward deployment, bilateral military alliances, and the development of missile defense systems continue to have some meaning. In the meantime, as the world searches for new approaches to address issues of the environment, ethnic division, transnational crime, poverty, AIDS, food security, and others, the United States also gropes for new raison d'être for its world leadership and global preponderance.

September 11: Effects on U.S. Foreign Policy and Responses of the International Community

When the terrorist attacks of September 11, 2001 happened, the debates on international security suddenly shifted from consideration of the post-Cold War configuration, into fathoming the "post 9/11" world. George W. Bush declared September 11 as the end of the post-Cold War era. It is a tribute to the success of U.S. hegemony that practically overnight, "international terrorism" which became the main threat to U.S. security was also accepted by many as the most serious challenge to world security.

It was easy enough to argue that what was bad for the United States was bad for the world, given the important role the United States plays in the world economically and politically, and in international security. That the most powerful nation could be so brazenly targeted underscored everyone's vulnerability to faceless and fearless enemies who set no limits to how far they would go to deliver a political message. As one American official expressed, "there is nothing so alarming as the idea that a nonstate actor could do so much damage."[4]

NATO responded quickly by invoking its Article V for the first time ever, declaring that the attack on the United States was an attack on all the members. Japan, also for the first time, agreed to mobilize its warships to support the U.S. military campaign against al-Qaeda and its Taliban supporters in Afghanistan, albeit not its Aegis cruisers and only in a noncombat role from a safe distance. China backed the relevant UN Security Council resolutions urging the international community "to take all necessary steps to respond to the terrorist attacks of 11 September 2001, which paved the way for the use of force against terrorism by the United States. It had in mind its own increasingly violent Muslim separatist movement in Xinjiang,

4 Statement by Ambassador Charles Salmon, former foreign policy adviser of the Commander-in-Chief, U.S. Pacific Command, during a lecture on "U.S. Policy on Terrorism," UP Asian Center, 13 December 2001.

which has been linked to Afghan militants. It also took action to help stabilize the situation along its borders with Afghanistan and Pakistan and prevent al-Qaeda operatives from crossing, exchanged intelligence information with the U.S., and subsequently contributed funds for the post-Taliban reconstruction in Afghanistan.[5] Russia similarly supported the American actions in Afghanistan, and did not resist the establishment of a U.S. military presence in its traditional sphere of influence in Central Asia, perhaps driven by its own anxiety over Chechen rebels who had also been engaged in terrorist activities in recent years.

Over a hundred coalition partners were eventually assembled under U.S. leadership for the response against terror. For one brief moment even, it appeared that the war on terrorism would change the unilateralist tendencies of the Bush administration, especially when it suddenly began to pay its dues to the United Nations and to seek cooperation from other countries. But eventually, in the debates in U.S. policy circles between the liberal multilateralists (personified by Sec. of State Colin Powell) on the one hand, and the realist-unilateralist camp (of Defense Sec. Donald Rumsfeld and Dick Cheney) on the other, it was the unilateralists who gained the upper hand (Hirsch 2002).

Since September 11, America's rhetoric has not only been tough against the terrorists, it also threatened to be tough on everyone else who did not immediately and completely back the strong U.S. response. Even constructive criticism from allies and friends has been preempted. Indeed, some dangerous premises and hasty conclusions were being drawn from 9/11, with serious implications for international security and U.S. foreign policy.

The first dangerous premise was Bush's by now famous words: "Either you are with us, or you are with the terrorists."

The simplistic statement could perhaps be best dismissed as rhetorical flourish, were it not for the serious consequences that fol-

5 Gill Bates, "September 11 and Northeast Asia: Change and Uncertainty in Regional Security," *The Brookings Review* 20, no. 3 (Summer 2002): 43-46, http://www.brook.edu/

lowed. Allies and friends, even putative ones, were called to march alongside Washington in the war effort in Afghanistan, no matter that the original military objective of ferreting out suspected al-Qaeda perpetrators expanded into the overthrow of a regime unfriendly to the United States, and no matter that the so-called search for justice began to seem more like an insatiable act of vengeance.

The fear of military reprisal and other consequences of being labeled terrorist or proterrorist by the United States government prevented important questions from being earnestly asked and answered. For instance, what are the real root causes and the driving force behind groups like al-Qaeda? Why is the United States the favorite target of international terror groups in the first place? Could U.S. actions and U.S. policy itself have been responsible for the disaffection against it felt by many in the Muslim world? Moreover, how effective can an Afghanistan-type of military and political intervention be against religious extremists, international terror groups and their alleged backers, particularly in terms of preventing future incidents by similarly desperate individuals and organizations?

There are many countries and peoples who are as much against terrorism as the Americans are, or likely even more so because of their more direct and frequent experience with violence from homegrown armed groups. But not all of them felt that the military strikes in Afghanistan were warranted, for the following reasons: (a) the lack of direct evidence at the time that Osama bin Laden was indeed responsible for the WTC and Pentagon suicide attacks; (b) the fear that the U.S. military response would punish many innocents, as indeed the reports of "collateral damage" show;[6] (c) concern that the military strikes as well as overthrow of the Taliban would alienate many Islamist groups even further, providing fodder for the extremists and creating a backlash effect; (d) the sentiment that the U.S. response was disproportionate to the injury it suffered (although the impact on the world of seeing the World Trade Center collapse on real time television was indeed huge); (e) a sense that the actions against the Taliban, and the actions against Saddam Hus-

6 One example is how American air strikes in Afghanistan on July 1 led to the accidental bombing of a wedding party in one village, killing 48 and injuring 117 civilians, mostly women and children (AP, "U.S. Probe Clears Gunship in Afghan Wedding Air Strike," Sept. 8, 2002).

sein and Iraq, including military strikes and forcing a regime change, constitute a violation of international norms of state sovereignty; and (f) the opinion that U.S. actions are no longer justifiable as part of its right of self-defense but are rather intended to advance other geopolitical goals.

Under the principle of "you are either with us or with the terrorists," which incidentally was woefully echoed by our own president when she accused critics of the R.P.-U.S. Balikatan military exercises of being "Abu Sayyaf lovers," none of the above reservations should be raised because doing so would ostensibly help the terrorist cause. Among the few brave world leaders who dared raise such issues, albeit belatedly, Mahathir of Malaysia stands out as saying:

"The powerful are bent on revenge rather than solutions. And so there will be no end to Muslim terrorism.

"The Answer does not lie in confrontation, in force, in a war to end all wars.

"(But) the answer lies in justice and fair play, in being sensitive, in being willing to step back and to admit mistakes and banish the idea that any one race has the monopoly of the right values, the right systems, and the right solutions to all the human ailments." (*PDI*, Sept. 9, 2002, A11)

A second risky conclusion made after 9/11 was that a terrorist threat to U.S. homeland security is a threat to the world peace and security.

It can perhaps be argued that any problem in any country has a potential for becoming a problem of the world, in the way that the illness of one part of the body affects the whole. Perhaps when that part of the body is as central to the entire system as the United States is to the world economy and international security, then the world does tend to take more notice. However, what makes the above proposition dangerous when applied to the United States is that by virtue of its power, the U.S. has an overwhelming capacity to dominate and desire to influence the agenda of the international community, if not by force of persuasion then by threats of withdrawal of support, as amply demonstrated in the past.

The manner in which international terrorism indeed began to dominate all kinds of international gatherings was understandable in the immediate aftermath of September 11.[7] That governments, anxious to prevent similar occurrences especially on their own ground, hurried to put in place security measures, better intelligence-gathering mechanisms, legislation to freeze terrorist access to resources, etc., whether or not at Washington's prodding, is also not surprising and in fact commendable. The concern over this second proposition instead stems from how, a year after, the attention of the international community and of governments across the globe is still being diverted from other equally if not more important and urgent world problems such as poverty, disease, the drug menace, and others that may matter more to a much bigger section of the world's population.

A third erroneous conclusion is that the U.S. bears the main or even the sole responsibility for wiping out terrorism across the world, and has the monopoly of the right approaches to do so, and that if necessary, therefore, the U.S. can and should go it alone.

This argument reveals the depth of the isolation and distance that the United States feels as the sole superpower cut so high above the rest, but it also reveals a deep-seated unilateralist impulse and a tendency to disengage.

When NATO invoked its Article V after 9/11, Defense Sec. Donald Rumsfeld sent word that this would not be necessary because, he argued, "the mission would define the coalition." Some would interpret this as outright contempt for NATO and Europe, and still others as a refusal to be bound by any multilateral arrangement that could restrain its initiative to deal with terrorism as it would (Hirsch 2002). Rather than build a broad antiterror coalition, and have the coalition define the mission, Washington would rather define the mission by itself, and then build the coalition that could serve its desired mission.

7 The APEC finance ministers spent much of a recent two-day meeting preparing an action plan against terrorist financing networks. "APEC Ministers Forge Anti-Terror Action Plan," (AFP, *The Philippine Star*, Sept. 8, 2002, 17).

Riding on the wave of international sympathy following the September 11 attacks and acquiescence to the overthrow of the Taliban, Washington has now trained its sights on removing yet another of its enemies from power—namely Saddam Hussein. The United States threatens to attack Iraq and to remove its leader in order to put a halt to his alleged support for terrorist groups and to forestall attempts to acquire weapons of mass destruction that could potentially fall into terrorist hands and target the United States. (The U.S. had not gone to Iraq and Saddam Hussein had not been taken prisoner when this article was written.-Ed.) However, evidence to support such assumption and allegations about Iraq has been scanty by all accounts, including the American CIA's.[8] Although the Iraqi regime was considered by many to be a potential threat to peace because of its possession of nuclear war material, which it had earlier refused to open to UN inspections, U.S. foes and friends alike doubt the legitimacy of U.S. efforts to institute a "regime change" in Iraq at this time.

French president Jacques Chirac has warned strongly against a U.S. go-it-alone attack, saying that war was the "worst possible solution" and that "everything must be done to avoid it" (Adams 2002). Germany opposed any invasion at all, while Italian Prime Minister Silvio Berlusconi said after a meeting with Putin in mid-October that "Iraq does not any longer have weapons of mass destruction because they have all been eliminated" (Watson n.d.). Pakistani leader Pervez Musharraf predicted "very negative repercussions around the Islamic world" of a U.S. invasion of Iraq. Turkey, Saudi Arabia, as well as NATO have also warned the U.S. against the consequences of waging war on Iraq (*PDI,* 31 Aug. 2002, A11).

Meanwhile, China opposes any U.S. action undertaken outside of the UN framework, where it sits on the Security Council. Russia's Putin expressed "serious doubts" about Bush arguments for striking Iraq, based on international law and "global political sense." Even Israeli Foreign Minister Shimon Perez commented that

8 The CIA said the probability of Iraqi president Hussein initiating an attack without provocation on the United States in the foreseeable future was "very low," according to a letter recently made public. Tabassum Zakaria, "CIA Says Iraqi Unlikely to Strike U.S. Unless Provoked," Reuters, Oct. 9, 2002)

an offensive against Baghdad "would not solve the Middle East's problems" while UN Sec. Gen. Kofi Annan was quoted as saying that a preemptive strike on Iraq would be "unwise" (*PDI,* Sept. 8, 2002). Only Britain and Australia, as expected, firmly aligned themselves with the U.S. desire to send troops to Iraq.

In Southeast Asia, the picture was mixed. Even during the overthrow of the Taliban, Mahathir of Malaysia had opposed any ASEAN resolution backing U.S. military action and argued that the group should only endorse a UN General Assembly resolution condemning terrorism. Indonesia's Megawati has especially been under pressure from conservative Muslim groups and politicians not to bow to U.S. interest, up until the Bali bombing on October 15 that killed nearly two hundred people. The political fallout from the bombing finally forced her to crack the whip against local terrorist organizations' suspected al-Qaeda links. The Philippines, on the other hand, has clearly tried to put up appearances of being firmly behind the United States both on Afghanistan and Iraq, but has been seen to waver in the face of opposition from below. National Security Adviser Roilo Golez added to the confusion through diplomatic double-speak when he said on October 14 that "Basically, the government is prepared to support the fight against terrorism, and to honor the process in the United Nations. It is also prepared to extend security, humanitarian, and political support to the U.S." (Pablo 2002).

Some commentators, whether supporters or critics of the U.S.-led antiterror campaign, have also warned about the U.S. focusing inordinately on military engagement rather than on political and diplomatic engagement. In addition, any decision to take preemptive military strikes in Iraq, and the emergence of a new U.S. strategic principle of "preemption" (replacing "containment" and "deterrence") raises important questions regarding the nature of the conflicts as well as the nature of the future international order.

The groundswell of opposition against a U.S. war in Iraq stems at least partly from the way Washington has in the past ignored the counsel of its allies, other great powers, and the representatives of the international community. As one observer noted, "Because the world gets only marching orders from Bush and not a common vision, it will be less inclined to follow them, especially if the United

States begins to take large-scale preemptive action against states such as Iraq" (Hirsch 2002). Henry Kissinger also wrote of the dangers of unilateralism: "The dominant trend in American foreign-policy thinking must be to transform power into consensus so that the international order is based on agreement rather than reluctant acquiescence."

But criticism is also directed at how facts have apparently been distorted by the U.S. government in its desire to overthrow Saddam Hussein. In particular, the U.S. has exaggerated the Iraqi leader's links with Osama bin Laden in order to legitimize its intended military assault on Iraq, as confirmed even by sources in Britain, France, and Czechoslovakia.[9] Another issue being raised is the apparent hypocrisy of U.S. policy regarding the proliferation of weapons of mass destruction, as it denies Iraq's right to possess nuclear weapons yet itself fails to abide by its obligations to disarm under the Nuclear Nonproliferation treaty. Moreover, some recall how the United States in the 1980s provided Saddam's army with satellite intelligence so that it could use chemical weapons against Iranian soldiers, and shipped seven strains of anthrax to Baghdad between 1978 and 1988. All because, although Saddam was seen as a monster, he was their kind of monster and ally against Iran. In much the same way, the United States had been partly responsible for the mushrooming of Islamic *mujaheedin* in Afghanistan as part of the anti-Soviet resistance. Little did they expect that their former allies would ultimately turn against them (Kristof 2002).

9/11's Impact on U.S. Relations with Major Asian Powers

In the emerging post-September 11 configuration, it is the role and relationships among the major powers that again remain uncertain. This section briefly considers the impact of 9/11 on China, Japan, Russia, and India and their respective relations with the United States.

China. Prior to 9/11, Bush did not have any clear-cut policy towards China, other than being critical of Clinton's strategic part-

9 Chirac told a Beirut newspaper that "no proof had been found" of a connection between al-Qaeda and the Iraqi regime. Prague denied an earlier report saying that Iraqi leaders had met in the city with Osama bin Laden at one time.

nership concept.[10] China did not loom as large in the consciousness of the Bush administration as it did in previous ones.[11] In contrast, Bush seemed to be very clear about what he wanted vis-à-vis Taiwan, stating very early on that the U.S. would be prepared to do "whatever it takes" to defend Taiwan, and in what may have been a Freudian slip even directly referred to Taipei as the "Republic of Taiwan." The obvious partiality for Taiwan and the lack of a strategic dialogue with Beijing were already seen as damaging to bilateral relations even prior to September 11.

While 9/11 is expected to have both positive and negative consequences for China and for U.S.-China relations, on the balance China appears to have suffered a strategic setback.[12] On the positive side, the terrorist threat has displaced the so-called "China threat" as the principal security concern of the United States, thus somewhat reducing strategic pressure on China. The relaxation of U.S. pressure on and criticism of China may also give the leaders in Beijing an excuse to step back and craft the desired constructive framework for a new relationship with the world's sole superpower. This is necessary considering that China needs smooth relations with the United States at this time of internal political transition and adjustment to economic challenges posed by the WTO (World Trade Organization).

The 9/11 attacks provided common security interests and objectives for Washington and Beijing to cooperate on, especially in light of the recent U.S. decision to consider the East Turkestan Independence Movement (ETIM) run by China's separatist Uighurs as a terrorist organization (Yuan 2002). In recent years, Muslim separatist movements in Xinjiang have increasingly resorted to setting up explosions, assassinations, and street fighting. Some attacks have even occurred in major cities like Beijing, Wuhan, and Guangzhou. Islamic fundamentalist elements in Central Asia, Afghanistan, and

10 Remarks of Elizabeth Economy on the Bush administration's policy towards China, delivered at a conference on "Dialogue, Competition and Cooperation in the Asia Pacific Region after China's Accession to WTO." Zhongshan University Center for Asia Pacific Studies, June 28, 2002.

11 Remarks of Robert Sutter, Prospects for Sino-U.S. Strategic Dialogue, delivered at a conference on the Zhongshan University Center for Asia Pacific Studies, June 28, 2002.

12 See also J. Mohan Malik, "Dragon on Terrorism: Assessing China's Tactical Gains and Strategic Losses after September 11," *Contemporary Southeast Asia* 24, 2 (August 2002).

the Middle East have reportedly trained some of the Uighur rebels responsible for these attacks. China's great concern over terrorism from Islamic extremists thus preceded 9/11, as seen in its persistent crackdowns against Uighur rebels and its initiative to establish the Shanghai Cooperation Organization together with Russia and several Central Asian Republics, which is mainly directed at neutralizing Islamic extremism along their common borders.

Washington's listing of the ETIM as terrorist adds legitimacy to Beijing's crackdown on Uighur separatism. Moreover, Washington had earlier been critical of China's human rights violations against the Uighurs, but after September 11, Washington became relatively silent on human rights issues as it itself began to flout international humanitarian law in the treatment of suspected terrorist prisoners in Guantanamo.[13]

On the negative side, the U.S. preoccupation with terrorism, an issue where China is in the ultimate analysis not considered a major player compared to countries in Central Asia, Southwest Asia and Southeast Asia, may likely continue the trend of the Bush administration's strategic indifference to China, relative to the attention Washington will give to enhancing military and security cooperation arrangements with its other Asian partners.

Moreover, the U.S. is moving more troops to Asia, seeing Asia as the second front on the war against terror and following the stabilization of Kosovo on the European front. The new U.S. presence in Uzbekistan and stronger links with Central Asia and Russia may be noncontroversial to China at this time, but already there have been expressions of concern that this, together with the existing bilateral alliances with Japan, Korea, and Australia, and the growing military ties with the Philippines and Indonesia, could eventually become part of a new U.S. policy of encirclement of China. China also reportedly does not want the Afghanistan reconstruction process to be "influenced too much by the international community."[14]

13 UN Human Rights champion Mary Robinson roundly criticized American treatment of said prisoners and decried how the campaign against terrorism under U.S. leadership has helped legitimize human rights abuses.

14 Reuters, "Concern over U.S. Plans for War on Terror Dominate Jiang Tour," April 7, 2002 (http://www.taiwansecurity.org/Reu/2002/Reuters-040702.htm), quoting Zhu Feng, director of Beijing University's International Security Program.

Also worrisome from China's strategic view is how the improvement in Russia-U.S. relations before and after September 11 may have undercut what had been a budding Sino-Russian dialogue that may have been intended to balance U.S. hegemonic influence.[15] Finally, any U.S. decision to attack Iraq or to unseat Saddam Hussein is bound to test relations with Beijing, because of how this would implicitly violate the principle of state sovereignty and possibly add precedent to future U.S. attempts to remove other unfriendly regimes. In April 2002, Jiang Zemin paid visits to Libya and Iran, both identified as rogue states and sponsors of terror by Washington, at a time when the U.S. was threatening to expand the antiterrorism campaign to Iraq. The visit was intended to show the U.S. that China did not entirely agree with the U.S.' views on terrorism and would, therefore, pursue an independent policy.[16]

As of this writing, however, within the UN Security Council, both France and Russia have expressed strong opposition to unilateral U.S. actions and to U.S. eagerness to go to war against Iraq, thus making it unnecessary for Beijing to state its own opposition to Washington in clearer terms. China's Foreign Ministry has instead stated that the Iraqi problem "should be solved in a political and diplomatic way within the framework of the United Nations" (Lam 2002). By fence-sitting on this crucial issue, China may figure that it can improve its standing in the eyes of the U.S., without sacrificing any of its own strategic objectives and foreign policy principles.

In general, one might expect that China will be prepared to go along with U.S. leadership in the campaign against terrorism, but not if it is undertaken unilaterally and in flagrant violation of international norms and processes; not if it becomes a blanket license for Washington to wage wars or subvert sovereign governments (Iraq now, China later?); and not if it provides a cover for Washington to legitimize an increase in permanent military presence, especially in

15 This was the assessment of Yang Jieman, vice president of the Shanghai Institute of International Studies, in his paper on Sino-U.S. Relations and its International Setting delivered at a conference on "Dialogue, Competition and Cooperation in the Asia Pacific Region after China's Accession to WTO." Zhongshan University Center for Asia Pacific Studies, June 28, 2002.

16 Reuters, "Concern over U.S. Plans for War on Terror Dominate Jiang Tour," April 7, 2002 (http://www.taiwansecurity.org/Reu/2002/Reuters-040702.htm), quoting Zhu Feng, director of Beijing University's International Security Program.

areas surrounding China. Chinese leaders likely realize, too, that the retreat to the backburner of the "China threat theory" is bound to be temporary rather than of long-term impact, because a rising China that remains a dissatisfied and aspiring great power, under the leadership of a Communist Party that continues to pursue socialism (no matter how minimal), will continue to be perceived as a challenge to U.S. global preponderance. China is after all seen as the only country in the world that is building up forces directed against the United States (Sutter 2002). Finally, the failure, thus far, to develop viable peaceful frameworks for addressing the Taiwan issue or the South China Sea disputes will ensure that the "China threat" theory remains.

India. Relations between Delhi and Washington had been difficult in the last fifty years, and only began to improve during the final years of the Clinton administration. Since perceptions of a China threat began to rise in Washington, there has been some talk about building a role for India as counterweight to Chinese influence in Asia. The U.S. criticized India for testing nuclear weapons in 1998, but India strategic planners as well as politicians tend to justify their country's nuclear build-up on the basis of a perceived nuclear threat from China, underscoring the prospects of long-term Sino-Indian rivalry that could be complicated by a U.S. factor.

India's attitudes towards terrorism and the U.S. antiterror campaign can only be understood in the context of its fifty-year conflict with Pakistan. India had long been trying to persuade the United States of the terrorist threat it faced in disputed Kashmir from militant *jihadis* or "freedom fighters," that it attributed to orchestration by the Pakistani Inter-Services Intelligence Directorate (ISI).[17] Since 1991, India had been providing the U.S. with intelligence information about Pakistani-sponsored terrorist activities and requesting Washington to declare Pakistan as a state-sponsor of terrorism. It was only after September 11 that the United States appeared to take India's concerns and the Kashmir issue more seriously, although U.S. interests dictated that it remain close to Pakistan on whom it relied for support in undercutting Taliban or al-Qaeda terrorist activity in neighboring Afghanistan.

17 Dennis Kux, "India's Fine Balance," *Foreign Affairs*, May/June 2002.

While economic relations with the United States will be important for India's future economic growth and global integration, its foreign policy posture is expected to remain independent from that of the United States. On the Iraq question, India's permanent representative to the UN. V.K. Nambiar expressed the view in October that "given the current configuration of circumstances, any undermining of the territorial integrity of Iraq could have unforeseen and destructive geopolitical implications. This could extend even beyond the region (Khrisnaswami 2002). He emphasized that the objective of UN weapons inspectors entering Iraq should be limited to disarmament, and that Iraq's effective compliance should be followed by the lifting of sanctions against it.

The recent U.S. decision to finally seek engagement with both India and Pakistan, not only for its antiterror objectives but also in relation to nuclear disarmament and the dispute over Kashmir may, however, add new uncertainties in triangular India-China-Pakistan relations. China, like the United States, supported Pakistan in the past because of their common distrust of India (then close to the Soviet Union), to the extent of helping Pakistan become a nuclear weapons state that it is now. But the prospect of a nuclear face-off between India and Pakistan over Kashmir as well as the perceived "Talibanization" of Pakistan's military government forced China to calibrate its support of Pakistan. On the other hand, the improving military ties between Pakistan and the U.S. itself may well undercut Beijing's influence over Karachi.

Japan. Japan, on the other hand, remains a firm ally of the United States and can be expected to continue its traditional role, since the Gulf War, of helping to bankroll U.S. military undertakings. Because it is an affluent country, highly urbanized, with dense population centers, and one that is closely associated with support for the U.S., there are fears that Japan could be an easy target for future terrorist actions. In the aftermath of 9/11, Japan extended unprecedented levels of military support to the United States' anti-terrorist efforts and its Afghan campaign, albeit in a noncombat role. In addition, it agreed to cochair with the United States the November 2001 Washington assembly on reconstruction assistance to Afghanistan. Japan is also expected to expand its nonmilitary role in Central Asian regional affairs, being the single largest donor of development aid to the region (Gill 2002).

In October 2001, the Japanese Diet launched a debate on what role Japan could play in the antiterror campaign given the parameters of its Peace Constitution. A counterterrorism law was passed that allows the Japanese Maritime Self-Defense Forces to provide logistics, supply, transportation, and communication assistance to U.S.-led forces, but requires Japanese vessels to operate only in noncombat areas (ibid.).

There is, however, also an increasing number of dissenting voices in Japan critical of its security dependence on the United States. Many politicians, including Prime Minister Koizumi himself, have also been known to support a stronger security role for Japan's Self-Defense Forces. The September 11 attacks somewhat heightened the debates on the "normalization" of Japan, where advocates of a "normal" Japan wish to see their country allowed to come to its own military defense, a de facto reversal of the Peace Constitution and a modification of the "nuclear umbrella" arrangement that it has with the United States.

Any prospect of an expanded security role for Japan has to consider the reaction of China and Korea, its immediate neighbors who continue to harbor strong suspicions of Japan's designs even fifty years after the Pacific War. Prior to mobilizing the Self-Defense Forces for the campaign in Afghanistan, Koizumi visited China and South Korea to explain his view of Japan's security role in the crisis and to issue apologies anew for Japan's aggression in the first half of the twentieth century.

An outstanding concern among Japanese analysts vis-à-vis U.S. foreign policy has been the perceived hardening of Washington's attitudes towards China and North Korea since Bush came into office. Increasing tensions between the U.S. and China as well as between the U.S. and North Korea would complicate Japan's own efforts to coexist peacefully with these two touchy neighbors. There is also Japanese resentment at the increasingly unilateral streak of U.S. foreign policy (especially after it junked the Kyoto Protocol) and its militaristic talk, including a Pentagon report that in many Japanese security specialists' eyes tended to exaggerate the military threat from China. In addition, Washington's call for possible military action against Iraq also unsettles Japan, which gets virtually all its oil from the Middle East and fears being dragged into the conflict (Struck 2002).

Russia. Osama bin Laden is today seen as a common enemy by Russia and the United States. He bankrolled the Afghan resistance to Soviet occupation in the 1980s and was thus considered friendly to U.S. interests at that time. He then turned against both, and became suspected of sponsoring terrorist activities targeting U.S. military presence in Africa and the Middle East, as well as bombings of civilian targets in Russia in 1999 that were mainly attributed to Muslim separatists in Dagestan and Chechnya.[18]

Still hounded by the Soviet Union's breakup and continuing efforts by certain groups to secede from Russia, Russian leaders equate terrorism with the activities of local separatists, and are extremely suspicious of external support for said groups. According to one American analyst, they see them both as "part of a broadly orchestrated plan from a single center of the terrorist international from Manila to Sarajevo" (Blank 2002). This argument was repeated during the hostage crisis in a Moscow theater in October 2002, when Putin said on television that the Chechen hostage-takers were acting in concert with bombers who had just blown up a tourist-filled bar in Bali and stores in Zamboanga (*CNN World News Report*, 25 Oct. 2002).

Putin has been trying to portray the war on Chechnya as an antiterrorist operation, in the same way that Bush had projected the overthrow of the Taliban as an extension of the hunt for terrorists.

Apart from its concern with terrorism, Russia may have used 9/11 to get back on the strategic map as far as its relations with the U.S. are concerned. It even considers itself the United States' strongest supporter in its antiterror campaign. Prior to 9/11, it had been sidelined following NATO's co-optation of its former satellite states, and severely criticized in the West for its record of violations of human rights in connection with its own campaigns against rebels in Chechnya.

18 Transcript of "Terrorism in Russia," Topic of Worldnet Washington Window, USIS, Sept. 27, 1999, with guests from the CSIS and Carnegie Endowment.

But by the summer of 2002, Putin began speaking of the possibility of Russia joining NATO, arguing that NATO should either consider admitting Russia or disband altogether.[19] While Moscow and Beijing had quite recently flirted with the idea of forming a partnership that would bring their voices together and increase their strategic clout vis-à-vis Washington, ultimately the choice made by Moscow appears to be to jump on the U.S. bandwagon rather than try to balance against it. The situation of essentially uncontested U.S. domination after September 11 provided the window of opportunity and the strongest justification for Putin to negotiate that shift in foreign policy posture.

Russia, however, looks at the Iraq issue as unrelated to its posture on terrorism. Russia has been Iraq's main ally in the UN Security Council during the last decade of negotiations and bickering over UN weapons inspections. It has, therefore, strongly opposed any threat of unilateral U.S. action against Iraq, or even a UN-sponsored resolution that may be interpreted as permitting the automatic use of force should Iraq fail to comply with the international body's standards for weapons inspection. Whatever the results of the current negotiations in the UN Security Council will be on the appropriate actions to take against Iraq, Moscow will want to preserve its vast economic interests there, including US$8 billion in Baghdad's debts, economic ties estimated to total US$40 billion, and hefty oil contracts. On the other hand, analysts point to the following possible trade-offs Washington might offer for Russia's abandonment of Iraq: full recognition of NATO membership, U.S. recognition of it as a market economy which will open greater trade privileges with both the U.S. and the global economy, and debt renegotiation with Western creditors.

In conclusion, we can see from the above discussion that 9/11 has given the United States an opportunity to define the kind of world leadership that it can exercise, particularly in light of the new types of security challenges that have emerged such as international terrorism. But a leader can only be as good as its ability to make others follow, and this is where the challenge for the United States

19 Kathleen Knox, "Russia: Will War on Terrorism Boost Russia's Chances of Joining NATO?" Radio Free Europe, http://www.rferl.org/.

now lies. Its vigorous response to the threat from terrorism, such as forcing other governments to show strong support in the absence of which the U.S. would be ready to act alone, has demonstrated a potential for bringing about realignments among the great powers of the Asia Pacific, including Russia, China, Japan, and India. But it is a response that increasingly appears bereft of reason or principle, if only because the leaders of America, the world's greatest power, have thrown considerations of international law and morality to the wind. The current message that the U.S. government delivers is that in the so-called war against terror, the use of force is legitimate, sovereignty and human rights are of no consequence, international cooperation would be nice but not necessary, and might makes right. If these are lessons that the other great powers—China, Japan, India, and Russia, for instance—will take to heart based on the example of the United States, then we can all live in dread of what the future international order will look like, and we will have U.S. leadership to thank for it.

References

Adams, Paul. 2002. "France makes strongest statement yet against war." *Toronto Globe and Mail.* Oct. 17.

Bates, Gill. 2002. "September 11 and Northeast Asia: Change and uncertainty in regional security." *The Brookings Review* 20, no. 3 (Summer): 43–46 at http://www.brook.edu.

Blank, Stephen. 2002. "Is Russia's war on terrorism the same as America's?" Bi-weekly Briefing (U.S. Army WatrCollege, Strategic Studies Institute). March 13.

Hirsch, Michael. 2002. "Bush and the world." *Foreign Affairs* (Sept./Oct. 2002).

Knox, Kathleen. N.d. "Russia: Will war on terrorism Boost Russia's chances of joining NATO?" Radio Free Europe. http://www.rferl.org.

Krisnnaswami, Sridhar. 2002. "India opposed to unilateral action against Iraq." *Hindu*. Oct. 17.

Kristof, Nicholas. 2002. "Revoling Dorr monsters." *New York Times*. Oct. 11.

Kux, Dennis. 2002. "India's fine balance." *Foreign Affairs* (May/June) http://www.foreignaffairs.org/search.

Lam, Willy Wo-Lap. 2002. "Beijing plays for gains on Iraq showdown." *CNN.com*. Sept. 11.

Pablo, Carlito. 2002. "NSC affirms RP support for U.S. vs. Iraq." *Inquirer News Service*. Oct. 14.

Philippine Daily Inquirer (PDI). 2002a. "Islamic, European nations step up bid to avert U.S. war plan." Aug. 31, A11.

———. 2002b. "Bush, Blair seek global backing for Iraq action." Sept. 8, A 9.

———. 2002c. "Mahathir message to the West: Revenge won't solve international terrorism." Sept. 9, A11.

Struck, Doug. 2002. "Japan, South Korea wary of following U.S.: Corporate scandals, administration's unilateral policies strain alliances." *Washington Post*. July 22, A12.

Watson, Roland. N.d. "America fails to woo allies."

Yuan, Jing-Dong. 2002. "Trying to make sense of China's Iraq policy." *Taipei Times*. Sept. 26.

Mindanao as the Next Battlefront: Implications on Philippine Security & R.P.–U.S. Relations

Angelo T. Reyes

Is Mindanao the next "battlefront?" Indeed, this subject cannot be taken lightly as it relates to our national security and sovereignty. National security is the concern of every Filipino. In light of the changes in the security environment, both internal and external, the scope of our national security has become a more comprehensive concept, encompassing other fields of interest. The achievement of our national objectives, however, is slowed down by the various challenges to our national security, foremost of which is terrorism.

Due to the rising resentment over the perceived difficulty of being given equal rights, some religious, cultural, and ideological groups have opted for the use of force to achieve the recognition of their causes and beliefs.

In response to these threats, the Armed Forces of the Philippines (AFP) sustains the conduct of Internal Security Operations. It is a comprehensive approach that seeks not only to defeat the armed components of the threats but also to address the socioeconomic, political, and cultural roots of these threats.

This strategy has reaped positive results. For instance, AFP operations against the local communist movement (LCM) have resulted in neutralizing several ranking cadres and dissident regulars. Furthermore, their strength decreased from over twelve thousand in 2001 to less than ten thousand during the first semester of 2002.

Meanwhile, the Moro Islamic Liberation Front (MILF) continues to carve out an independent Islamic state in the region.

Nevertheless, our peaceful policy has resulted in a significant decline in MILF-related armed incidents. As of the first semester of 2002, their strength decreased from the yearend 2001 figure of 12,570 to 12,450.

The Misuari breakaway group emerged as a threat after it launched a series of attacks on military units and detachments in Sulu on 19 November 2001. Since the start of the year, however, the group has been inactive and their strength decreased from over 3,200 last year to about 360.

The new security environment, however, demands that we take on an even greater responsibility. As we continue to resolve our internal conflicts, we should also allow our attention to extend to the vital concerns of global security. We have a stake in what goes on in the rest of the world. The peace, freedom, and security of one nation are important to its people as it is to everyone else around the world.

The events of 9/11 force us to evaluate our national security policies and procedures. These were not attacks on just one nation anymore, but on the global community. Therefore, we must respond as a community.

Furthermore, since the United States pinpoints connections between the al-Qaeda and the Abu Sayyaf Group (ASG), we are compelled even more to act in order to stamp out these terrorists.

First surfacing in 1991, the ASG claims to be fighting for a separate Muslim state governed by the Shariah. In the light of rampant kidnappings and beheadings, however, other Muslim groups have been quick to denounce any connection between their pursuit of separatism and the ASG.

Yet the link between the ASG and the al-Qaeda network of Osama bin Laden cannot be discounted. This is proven by the start-up money used to fund the beginnings of the ASG: so-called scholarship programs facilitated the sending of Muslim Filipino rebels to bin Laden's terrorist training camps in Afghanistan.

The ASG has brought havoc in Mindanao especially in the past two years. This prompted the Philippine government to utilize all possible means of eradicating this pressing threat to our national security. In fact this year's R.P.-U.S. joint military exercises are held in Mindanao to make the training scenarios more realistic and relevant to the actual perceived threat.

The Balikatan has been conducted in Luzon and Visayas in the past years with the involvement of thousands of military personnel from the United States and the Philippines. The most recent exercise, Balikatan 02-1, involves some 660 U.S. forces; out of these, only 160 U.S. personnel are directly involved during the training in Basilan, the site of so much fear and terror caused by the ASG.

Enjoying the support of bin Laden's network, the ASG fearlessly echoed al-Qaeda's determination to bring chaos and destruction to the Western world. This malevolent purpose is heightened by the recent active Philippine- U.S. military arrangements.

A common assumption as revealed by the onslaught of ugly reports is that Mindanao is an area that cradles terrorists known for savagery. The U.S. then came to Mindanao to help hunt down these ruthless bandits and end the terror that they sow in the shortest time possible. All these unfortunate occurrences and unfounded theories have led some to believe that Mindanao is likely to be the next battlefront of terrorism, the next site of U.S. outrage against terrorism. But is it?

The mutual exchange of support between the Philippines and the United States after 9/11 fuelled further the belief of not a few analysts who describe the Philippines as an American "frontline state in the war on terrorism." But are we? The answer may be made clearer if we take a historical look at our relations with the United States.

The Philippines and the United States became allies when they concluded the Mutual Defense Treaty (MDT) in 1951. Over the years, it has become the foundation and consideration in the pursuit of our external defense objectives. It serves as a commitment between the two sides as defense partners to respond in the event of an armed attack by foreign forces on metropolitan territories, Armed Forces, public vessels or aircraft of either countries. The MDT is bolstered by a number of bilateral defense and security arrangements, which include the Military Assistance Agreement of 1947 and the Mutual Defense Assistance Agreement of 1953.

R.P.-U.S. defense relations is further enhanced by the conduct of regular military exercises in the fields of disaster relief, humanitarian assistance, and peace-keeping operations, operational planning, control, tactics, and community relations projects.

Balikatan is another joint R.P.-U.S. military-to-military exercise that started out as a Navy-to-Navy exercise in 1981. It was intended to test concepts, doctrines, and plans developed by the MDB in scenarios where the MDT may be invoked.

Balikatan was designed to enhance combat readiness and interoperability of both forces. Through the years, the Philippines provided the venue for the activity while the U.S. provided the support materials needed such as fuel, training ammunition, civic action equipment, and materials. Earlier exercises included operational cross training such as amphibious landing, airborne and jungle warfare, and SAR (search and rescue) operations.

Eventually, the exercise expanded with the inclusion of bigger forces, and became an annual event. When the R.P.-U.S. bases agreement was not renewed and the U.S. military bases were pulled out in 1992, the legal protection accorded to U.S. military forces also ceased leading to the suspension of the Balikatan exercises in 1996. There were attempts to come out with Status of Forces Type Agreements (SOFA), which eventually resulted in what is known as the Visiting Forces Agreement, or VFA.

With the unanticipated terrorist attack on the World Trade Center in New York City on September 11, 2001, a new threat to global security was posed. In a split second, the inconceivable threat of terrorism plagued not only the United States but the whole world as well. This ferocious assault against a superpower only implies that even titans such as the U.S. are no longer safe from the vicious claws of terrorism. Hence, a new security environment needs to be defined.

The tragic incident definitely rekindled the vigor in R.P.-U.S. diplomatic and military relations. When the United States called for global support to combat terrorism, the Philippines immediately responded by granting the United States over-flight rights for American military aircraft. The Philippines also offered Clark Air Field and Subic Bay Naval Base for use by the International Coalition against terrorism as transit points or staging areas for troops fighting the war against terrorism in Afghanistan.

Owing to the changed international security environment after September 11, the Philippines again embarked on a military exercise with the United States to strengthen and fortify our Armed Forces in the fight against terrorist groups such as the Abu Sayyaf.

Among the many bilateral military exercises between the Philippines and the United States, it is Balikatan 02-1 that is the most well-known and controversial because the exercises were held in Mindanao.

Though there are qualms that such exercise is a prelude to the return of U.S. bases in the country and that it is designed for combat operations, it should be made clear that as a matter of policy, no U.S. permanent basing and support facility shall be established in the country except for temporary structures, such as troop billets, classrooms, and mess facilities which will be utilized only for the duration of the exercise. Furthermore, the terms of reference have explicitly stated that the exercise does not involve actual combat operations. All activities during the exercise shall be consistent with the Constitution and other existing legal parameters in force.

The American government reciprocated our strong support for the International Coalition Against Terrorism. Pres. George Bush promised a $92.3 million support for the AFP. This amount is to be used for the procurement of military equipment which is expected to enhance not only the AFP's ability to counter terrorism but also to increase its wherewithal to fight local insurgents and protect our territory and exclusive economic zones.

Over the years, R.P.-U.S. defense and military relations have been very constructive for the AFP. First, this relationship serves as a conduit that fills in the technological gap between the AFP and the U.S. forces. The AFP currently lacks modern devices necessary to raise the effectiveness of its operations. Through military exercises, Filipino soldiers acquire the necessary training, experience, and knowledge in the use of such military contraptions to be acquired in the future.

It also serves as a force multiplier. Through a series of training activities like the Balikatan, the AFP is afforded with an avenue for the advancement of skills and capabilities especially in areas that require planning, readiness, and interoperability among branches of service and with other friendly forces.

Bilateral confidence building is also engendered through military exercises. Confidence-building measures that were established through periodic joint military exercises have become necessary for the cultivation of cooperative behavior in defense and security between the Philippines and the United States.

After the terrorist attacks in the U.S. homeland, cooperation in the U.S.-led global campaign against terrorism is but logical. This cooperation entails not only military alliance but economic cooperation as well to effectively address not only the terrorist act per se but also, more importantly, its root causes.

In her visit to the United States, President Arroyo was able to forge an intensified economic linkage with the United States. President Bush asked the U.S. Congress to grant $25M to the Philippines as an emergency supplemental budget for 2002.

The renewed vigor of R.P.-U.S. defense relations provided for the significant reestablishment of the American presence not only in the Philippines but in the whole of Southeast Asia. This also granted the enhancement of American network of strategic bilateral alliances, which is essential in serving as a counterweight against any feasible aggressor in the region.

The dawning of this new millennium fosters both challenges and opportunities for all states and governments. The U.S. and the Philippines are faced with the complex task of uplifting and enriching the living and social conditions of their peoples and the affirmation of their sovereignty. Now that there manifest apparent opportunities to contend with poverty, forging closer links with the rest of the world has become, more than ever, essential for our national security.

Although these challenges are not yet grievously destabilizing, there emerges a compelling need for the firm resolve of the entire nation to contain and prevail over these challenges. We should, therefore, put premium on the optimal use of our bilateral defense arrangements with other countries, not only with the United States, to enhance our security.

Which leads us back to the basic question: Is Mindanao the next "battlefront" of terrorism? Certainly not. For us Filipinos, Mindanao represents a more important challenge—it is the arena of development, peace, and harmony. And in this battleground, our government is vigorously pursuing peace and prosperity.

We, in the Department of National Defense, believe that safeguarding our nation's security and sovereignty is a collective effort by the government, the military, and the citizenry. You know as well as we do that our vision of a peaceful and progressive nation can only be realized and attained if each of us fulfills our part of the deal.

I remember the poet William Butler Yeats once observed, "In dreams begin responsibility." Those of us who dream of peace and progress are called upon to do our share in building a strong republic. Each of us has the responsibility to shape the future of our nation.

Religious Differences and Political Conflict

José S. Arcilla, S.J.

In 2002 a nun in India was convicted of having illegally converted some Dilats to Roman Catholicism, and sentenced to six months imprisonment. In 1989, she had already been, with a Belgian priest, convicted of the same crime and fined £6. Church superiors claimed she could not have violated the existing laws, since there could not have been any religious conversion as the Dilats have no religion. The case is on appeal, although we have received no further news about it.

This incident, unfortunately not isolated where Roman Catholicism is the religion of a minority of the population, exemplifies a key issue in this volume. There is a need for a corporate examination of conscience to understand the tragedy of September 11, 2001, in the hope of avoiding a similar incident in the future. We need to examine two visions of life that ideally are complementary, but historically have occasioned violent conflicts. Observers agree that the bloody 9/11 was at bottom a desperate expression of unrelieved poverty and hopelessness, for even the newly coined word "globalization" implies in the opinion of many merely a sophisticated exploitation of the marginalized.

Observers also agree that an equally violent reaction will worsen the situation, for more than military action, it was a cry of anguish—justified or not is another question—to satisfy the essential human need for a just share of the world's goods. Plotted and executed by followers of the Ku'ran against those of the Christian

Bible, the temptation is to view it as part of the differences between Islam and Christianity. Were it as simple as that, the solution would be much easier.

Political conflict stemming from religious differences has characterized human history. Paradoxically, they worsened with the appearance of Christianity. Such violence was not usual in ancient pre-Christian societies, mainly because the supreme political leader was also the supreme religious leader, or high priest. But with Christianity a new view of life appeared, threatening the old.

Suspicious of the exclusivist conduct of the Jews, the Roman Empire was notorious for its anti-Semitism and persecuted the Jews. The latter observed a special moral code and cult, and their material success aroused at least jealousy that quickly worsened into hostility. History records show that in 71 A.D., the Roman legions wiped away Jerusalem, the sacred Jewish city.

Mistaken for Jews, the early Christians also suffered the ire of the Roman Empire. But only one emperor, Decius (249–51 A.D.) decreed universal anti-Christian persecution and other anti-Christian persecutions were neither widespread at any single time, nor were of equal intensity or violence. We cannot tell how many victims there were; the modern science of hagiography has lessened their number.

Historians argue about the legal basis for the Christian persecutions, and the question persists why such a legally oriented government as the Roman Empire could have, not initiated, but at least countenanced such a reaction. The new Christian moral code and the exclusivist Christian cult in which only the initiates were allowed to participate, as in the case of the Jews, aroused suspicion, and hatred for the Christians expressed itself in crude caricatures, such as that of Christ with a donkey's head nailed to the cross. Popular feeling led to popular riots, forcing the state to intervene. The Christians were charged with at least two crimes, *odium generis humani* (hatred for the human race), and lèse majesté (affront to the power and majesty of public authority), especially since the Christians absolutely refused to worship the emperor or serve in the imperial army. Refusal to worship Dea Roma threatened the very life of the empire, and the only reaction was to remove such a danger.

In a deeper sense, Rome had to combat the new Christian ideology, which was incompatible with the old. Society dies when it has served its purpose, and its inner vitality is gone. There is no need for an external force to destroy it, because society has become an empty shell without any substance. The Greco-Roman culture had reached its apex, beyond which human talent could not go. A new vitality was needed to infuse life, but it could not be the same as the old. Exhausted humanity needed something else, which Christianity offered. To continue existing then, Rome either had to accept Christianity and in the process be changed, or reject it. Rome rejected Christianity.

The severest persecutions occurred under the more capable Roman emperors of the second century. Some dismiss incidents like the persecution initiated by Nero (54–68 A.D.), an apparently psychologically unbalanced emperor, who was looking for a scapegoat for the burning of Rome. But Diocletian's move against Christianity in the first half of the third century was the most systematic, the cruelest, and the bloodiest. He had inherited power when the empire was about to collapse, and he tried to avoid the disaster. All in all, there were only 6 years of persecution during the first century, 86 during the second, and 24 during the third century. But history is witness to the unconquerable vitality of the Christian vision of life.

The Middle Ages saw a number of heterodox movements, but Western Europe was, in someone's phrase, a religious and political "monolith." The execution of a person like John Hus (1374–1415) could have resulted from inchoate nationalist sentiments, but hardly due to political conflicts, as we understand the term. There were relatively few instances like it in the Middle Ages.

The religious wars of the late sixteenth and early seventeenth centuries are another example of political conflicts because of religious differences, but this time it was not between Christian and non-Christian; rather it was between Christians of clearly variant political views.

The breakup of the medieval reich led to several Burgundian kingdoms, although the traditional nobility sought to revive the old unity of the Holy Roman Empire. Charles V (1517–1556) succeeded in forging some kind of legal unity at the Diet of Augsburg (1548) when he approved the "United Provinces" of northern Europe. It was, however, a precarious union for individualistic tendencies remained. Some cities continued to enjoy their privileges and immunities, provincial deputies claimed practical independence from the central power, and the high nobility were as powerful as the emperor.

Philip II (1556–1589), son and successor of Charles, centralized his government and tried to impose political and religious uniformity. He failed, and in 1581, the Netherlands declared their independence from Spain. The Dutch were the first capitalists in Europe, intellectuals and convinced Calvinists, and they fought for freedom from the imperial ordinances, or *plakats*.

A similar development occurred in France. The Bourbons, mainly Calvinist converts, and the Guises, orthodox Catholics, fought to control the crown. The economic crisis of the sixteenth century worsened an already complex situation. The French nobility sought, and in several instances succeeded, in secularizing church property, which led to violence. We should not forget that the earlier Lutheran movement had found supporters among the German nobility who saw in it an occasion to despoil the traditional Church of its properties, even violently.

Even non-Christian groups had been fighting to defend traditional convictions. The Shiites did not always see eye-to-eye with the Sunnites. In the late-fifteenth and early-sixteenth centuries, the Ottomans were pitted against the Shiites in what today would be Iraq. In the time of Suleiman I the Magnificent (1495–1566), the Ottomans lost Mesopotamia, but Abbas I the Great (1557–1628) led Persia to a golden age of unprecedented wealth and extended its frontiers.

Learning from his predecessors' mistakes, Akbar (1542–1605) established a solid base for a new state we know as the Great Mogul Empire. What he accomplished shows that religious differences do not necessarily lead to political conflicts. He promoted peaceful coexistence among subjects of different religious persuasions. He did away with the differences between Brahmins and Muslims, allowed marriage between them, and imposed Hindu as the official tongue. As a key element in the religious program he envisioned for a unified state, he himself abjured Islam in 1852. And to this end, he cancelled the tax on non-Muslims and published an edict of religious toleration in 1593.

The Europeans obtained a foothold in Asia only on sufferance and under conditions local potentates imposed on them. European presence in Asia was, of course, a mixed blessing. At least it helped to bring an end to chronic fighting among mutually hostile local leaders, and unified them in larger political entities; but the negative effect is dramatized in the death of Christian converts, whom the Roman Catholic Church now honors as "martyrs."

Islamic traders from the Middle East had preceded the Christians to Asia, but no significant conflicts or political turmoil ensued. They were mainly traders doubling as preachers of the prophet's religion, but apparently without seeking local political control, outside of imposing a way of life the Ku'ran demanded. Both among the Muslims and the Filipinos Spain subsequently Hispanized, we see a sociopolitical reorganization occasioned by religion. But we observe in history that religious conflicts occur only where society has reached a certain level of political and cultural sophistication.

The ancient trade routes between the Mediterranean and China had been disrupted by Tamerlane's advance late in the fourteenth century, but in the next century the Portuguese and the Spaniards restored communications between the East and the West.

Following the footsteps of St. Francis Xavier, the Portuguese Jesuits quickly transformed Macau into a door through which the Europeans introduced Christianity into China. In 1598, Michele Ruggieri (1543–1607) and Matteo Ricci (1552–1610) entered the imperial capital. Their learning and science won over the reclusive Chinese, who officially accepted Christianity in 1610.

The key to the Jesuit success in China was Ricci's scholarship and admiration for the ancient Chinese cultural heritage. He studied the Chinese literary treasures and became a Mandarin among the Chinese Mandarins. And he concluded that the ancient Chinese tradition of honoring dead ancestors and other traditional Chinese customs were merely social, not religious practices. Hence, with a clear conscience, baptized Chinese could continue honoring their ancestors in the traditional manner. Christianity posed no threat and did not mean turning against one's self. He proved that the Gospel did not destroy what the Chinese had, but perfected it instead. In no time at all, the Jesuits had established 300 churches with about fifty thousand new Christians.

But others disagreed. Equally zealous to spread Christianity and save the millions of pagans in continental China, the Dominicans and the Franciscans also tried and succeeded in entering China. They were shocked at the Jesuit method, which they described as placing God and Belial on the same altar. And with all their might, they pressured and fought the Jesuits in the so-called Chinese rites controversy, until, partially informed, Rome disapproved the alleged idolatry the lax Jesuits allowed among their converts.

The Roman decision reached China in 1704. Emperor K'ang Hsi, who first allowed the missionaries to preach Christianity openly was the first to ban it, and he deported the missionaries. Anti-Christian persecution worsened in the time of his successors, especially during the rule of Chia Ch'ing (1796–1820). Several died as martyrs, which most of them desired anyway, but their misplaced orthodoxy destroyed the initial wave of Christianity in China.[1] One now questions whether the continued presence of the Christian religion and the values it preaches would have made a better China today.

Not too different is the story of Christianity in Japan, which St. Francis Xavier introduced. The Jesuits who went there after him consolidated his initiatives and not a few from the *daimyo* class became Christians. This was a loss of face for the rest of the Japanese nobility and a decrease in the temple revenue. Purposely or not, the Christianized daimyos turned out to be instrumental in the conversion of their fiefdoms, much like the European's political practice in the seventeenth century, "cuius regio eius religio."

Battered by a storm on its way from Manila to Acapulco in 1596, the galleon *San Felipe* found safety in a Japanese harbor. The crew and the passengers were jailed, their goods confiscated. Imprudently, its pilot showed a map and boasted how Spain had conquered

1 Literature on the Chinese rites controversy is abundant. A good bibliographical guide would be the pertinent volumes of Streit-Dindinger, *Bibliographia Missionaria* (Romae, 1936 ff). The article in *Dictionaire de Théologi Catholique* 22:2364–91, is still the standard account. For a start, see Francis A. Rouleau, S.J., "Maillard de Tournon, Papal Legate at the Court of Peking," *Archivum Historicum Societatis Jesu* 31 (1962): 264–323 or George H. Dunne, S.J., 1962, *A Generation of Giants* (Notre Dame, Ind.), especially pp. 159–89.

the Americas and the Philippines, first through missionaries, and then through soldiers. Whether sheer braggadocio or simple naïveté led the pilot to try to impress his captors, we cannot say; but he not only unleashed a wave of hostility, but also confirmed the Japanese fear of foreigners, a fear that exploded in the Christian persecutions of the seventeenth century.

We can say almost the same thing of Korea, where Confucianism, Buddhism, and Taoism were the three spiritual currents. Korea had banned foreign travel, except to Peking to pay the tax. But Japanese soldiers who had entered the country during the invasion of 1597 brought some Christian writings with them, and the first Korean Christians were baptized in the last decade of the sixteenth century. Some of them died in Japan during the Christian persecutions there.

In other words, wherever Christianity was first introduced, new values threatened traditional ways. Significantly, the first Manila Synod convened to solve the initial dislocation immediately following the conquest of the Philippines and declared that if pagan chiefs allowed the spread and the practice of Christianity, they should not be deposed, even if they refused Christian baptism. For to repeat the Christian Gospel does not deprive one of what one has, but improves and perfects it.

The initial contact between the Cebuanos and Magellan in 1521 is well-known. Asked who would succeed him, Chief Humabon of Cebu answered that since he had no sons, his nephew, who married the chief's oldest daughter, would thereby become the crown prince. Innocently the chief added that "when the fathers and mothers grew old, they received no further honor, but their children commanded them." The Christian in Magellan reacted and he immediately explained that in his Christian society, even the old and the sickly elders were respected. God, he added, "had commanded us to honor our fathers and mothers, and that whoever did otherwise was condemned to eternal fire." The idea, novel and totally unexpected, pleased the Cebuano chief, who asked for teachers to instruct them further. With his followers, Humabon subsequently received baptism.

In 1564, forty-five years later a squad Legazpi had ordered to avenge the death of a Spanish soldier came back with some prisoners, among them the niece of Chief Tupas of Cebu. Upon learning who she was, Legazpi sent her attendant back to summon the chief to a parley and, if he wanted, lead the captives home. Tupas did not come, but his brother, the girl's father, did, with six men whom he was offering, with himself, as slaves to Legazpi for his daughter's release. The latter declined the offer and asked if they wanted their prisoners back. They, of course, did, and Legazpi had their girl led out, dressed in clothes that befitted her noble rank, to her father's utter amazement. That war captives should receive such humane treatment was totally unheard of. And it won over the girl's father, who promised he would convince his brother, the chief of Cebu, to make peace with the Spaniards or he would have him killed, as he had men to do it for him.[2]

Hardly mentioned in traditional Philippine historiography, these two incidents, which incidentally are a window to pre-Hispanic Philippine culture, marked the start of the Spanish presence in the Far East. But, of course, the Spaniards conquered the Philippines piecemeal, and they had to consolidate their individual military victories before the indigenous leaders submitted to foreign rule. After their initial surrender, the local chiefs in and around Manila tried to oust the newly installed conquerors, but with superior weapons and military tactics the Spaniards always bested their opponents. In due time, there was hardly any serious challenge to Spanish rule in the country.

Perhaps, more than in the Americas, Christianity consolidated Spanish presence in tribal Philippines. There had been an indigenous cult and religion, but instead of being regarded as a threat, the new Christian values summed up in the story of the crucifixion offered a superior spiritual vision that won the people over, except the politically more sophisticated Muslim Magindanaos and Sulus in southern Philippines. Even then, the subsequent Moro-Hispanic rivalry in the Philippines was neither exclusively a political nor a religious conflict.

In 1587, the Spanish authorities in Manila uncovered what is described as the first serious attempt to oust the Spaniards by a group headed by Magat Salamat. They contacted a Japanese adventurer

2 Detailed report by Esteban Rodriguez, pilot of the Legazpi expedition to the Philippines, 1566: *Colección de documentos inéditos,* 2a serie (Madrid, 1886) 2: 425–26.

who tried to smuggle men and arms for their cause. For three nights he gathered his leaders, and amid generous quaffs of *basi*, celebrated their future triumph. In these nightly revelries, they recited their litany of grievances and pledged to help one another, "if they wanted to see their estates free, *for they were no longer held in fear or obeyed as formerly, they no longer had slaves or gold, but on the contrary, they had been impoverished, languished daily in jail, their wives had been taken away from them and given to those who claimed they had married them first*" (Porra Camuñez 1908, 71–74). They also contacted the Pampangos, who refused to join them when they failed to agree on who would exercise authority after their victory. Finally they sent arms to entice the sultan of Borneo to join their revolt; but their agent let slip a careless word in Mindoro where he had stopped to recruit followers. The plot was uncovered, the trial was swift, and punishment was ruthless.[3]

The incident was the first and last serious attempt to oust the Spaniards from the Philippines. But it was not a religious problem; rather, the plotters wanted to return to the old dispensation of the pre-Hispanic society when they were its undisputed leaders.

The Magindanaos were seafarers who lived on trade at an age when trade was just one step removed from piracy. Seafarers grabbed what they could, and trafficked if they had to. Moreover, though fertilized by the free-flowing Pulangi River, their homeland produced hardly anything of commercial value. It gave them rice and sago for their food, but for international exchange they had to go elsewhere. And the Visayas in the north had precisely what they wanted, a commodity of great value, which was both self-propagating and easily obtainable: human beings. The Magindanaos and the Sulus were just settling down to the profitable business of supplying the slave markets of Southeast Asia when the Spaniards arrived. As for the Spaniards, having conquered the Visayas and Luzon, they tried to impose their rule on Magindanao and Sulu by the same methods. They failed.

3 Wenceslao E. Retana, *La primera conspiración separatista* (Madrid, 1908); Antonio de Morga, *Sucesos de las Islas Filipinas* (Retana ed., Madrid, 1909), 405, n 49; Francisco Colin, *Labor evangélica* (Pastells ed., Barcelona, 1900) 1: 172–74, n 2; Horacio de la Costa, *Jesuits*, 111–16.

We cannot detail the incidents in that long Moro-Hispanic rivalry in the Philippines, but we cannot say they were due to religious differences. The Muslims seemed not to have tried to expel the Spaniards from the Philippines—if indeed they wanted to. On the one hand, the Spanish government did not have sufficient means to rein in the unconquered south, while, on the other hand, as hinted at, it was a question of their socioeconomic survival that energized the Muslims to resist any Spanish advance.

In the middle of the seventeenth century, a peace treaty between Manila and Magindanao was signed. But peace was costly, and the successor realized that the garrisons could not be maintained at the same time that the government had to be ready for the more serious danger of the Dutch who threatened the Spaniards. Some kind of an understanding with the Muslims was needed, and the Jesuit Alejandro López negotiated a peace treaty for ten years. But the Muslims soon became restive, since sea rovers whose slave raiding provided them livelihood could not be expected to settle down to peaceful farming. And so, minor irritants and violations of the peace treaty occurred.

In 1655, López was back in Magindanao to protest certain breaches of the peace. Unfortunately, though the Jesuit might have been right, he said something that irritated Sultan Kudarat and the rest of his court. Father López recited a long list of violated terms of the treaty, and he bravely but politely said that Kudarat had not fulfilled the promise to allow Christian missionaries in his territory. But López let fall what was uppermost in his mind, when he added that actually religious differences were at the bottom of all their quarrels, and so "the simplest way" to end them was for Kudarat and his people to embrace Christianity. Kudarat fell into a rage. As Fr. Horacio de la Costa put it in his usual masterly style, "the missionary had got the better of the diplomat." Not much later, a lance killed the Jesuit turned government emissary. In a letter to the sultan of Sulu, Kudarat wrote, "I send you word that we have put to death the fathers. They wished to make Christians of us, and so we killed them. It will be good hereafter for us to act in concert for the defense of our faith."[4]

4 H. de la Costa, *Jesuits*, 452–60, and the primary sources he cites in n 27, p. 666.

With López's death also died the immediate prospects for peace between the Philippine Muslims and the Philippine colonial government. And the Muslim raids continued, until steam gunboats and the Jesuits reopened the Tiruray mission in Cotabato in 1861. A famine in Magindanao in 1872 unexpectedly helped the Christian cause, for the Muslims were forced to barter their slave children for food. The Jesuits grabbed the opportunity, and with funds from donors in Manila and Spain, ransomed the children, for whom they built an orphanage to raise them as Christians. And Tamontaka became a Christian oasis in the midst of Islam. Soon, aside from religious instruction, pioneering studies of Mindanao's flora and fauna, local idioms, and other aspects of life on the island were undertaken (Arcilla in *PS* 26 [1978]: 16–34; *PS* 27 [1979]): 126–97).

But criticism was open and frequent. The missions had not expanded beyond their limited periphery, and there were hardly any Christian conversions. A number in Manila wanted strong-arm methods to force the Muslims either to accept Christian baptism or leave. Fr. José Ignacio Guerrico, one of the first Jesuits in Tamontaka, had an answer, which all of us will do well to consider.[5]

Against the majority opinion, he believed the Jesuits, and everyone else should consider the Muslims, not just as possible friends, but as people who deserved to be treated with charity. There were indeed stories of Muslim treachery and cruelty, but he insisted that one could not generalize or jump to unfounded conclusions, and instead check the veracity of such tales. Suspicion leads to hatred, hatred to hostility, he remarked. As the means to accomplish some good to the Muslims—and to anybody else—he listed five points.

First, no one should despair of the Christianity of the Muslims, for it was a spiritual task whose success did not depend on them but on divine grace. Rather than discouragement, there were "reasons to take courage believing that the work will not be all wasted. The hope of good results encourages one to work and fires one's zeal, while lack of confidence discourages or inhibits...from toiling for what is useful, and diminishes or kills zeal."

5 See the Guerrico letters translated and edited by José S. Arcilla, S.J., in *Kinaadman* 3 (1981): 137–52; 4 (1982): 203–57.

Second, one should desire and form a strong resolve to work for the good of the Muslims whenever and wherever possible, with all the means that "present themselves and looking for others within reach."

Third, such openness will show what was actually possible "at least to prepare for the future." But one must start by "loving them with a special love and sympathizing with their unfortunate lot." Inevitably, such attitudes will express themselves in their speech, their faces, and an active concern for them. Naturally, one should learn their idiom.

Fourth, one should try to win the trust and affection of their leaders.

And fifth, prudence in one's speech when speaking about the Muslims, and one should beware of badmouthing them, for, "besides being totally useless, it would, if passion enters, make them look on the non-Muslims with hatred."

More importantly, perhaps, than these five points, Father Guerrico totally disagreed with the idea of "cleaning" Magindanao, the home of the Muslims, and peopling it with other people. By what right should one try to displace them? Even if they voluntarily left, where would they go? Would they be better off in the new place? And what guarantee was there that in that new place no one would try to oust them?

We note the same phenomenon when, hearing of the gold in the Mountain Province in northern Luzon, the Spaniards tried to occupy the place by, as one might expect, opening Christian missions among the Igorots. The Spaniards failed. Faced with the prospect of at least becoming Christians, the Igorots reacted with force, until the Manila government gave up the attempt (Scott 1977).

One notices in all of these incidents in the Philippines, as well as in the rest of Asia, that tension and violent skirmishes occurred when a new set of values threatened an accepted way of life. For religion and its complex of values are essentially a vision of life and life is always structured according to common ways of acting—or, in simple terms, in a political setup supported by laws.

Laws are needed for community life, for conscience alone is a weak guide to the good life. At the same time, law or a political constitution, no matter how well conceived, does not provide the moral strength to implement it. Laws indeed define what is wrong or what is correct. But it is conscience structured in external religious practices that energizes us to live according to that criterion and, therefore, is the cohesive force of every state. Change this with a new set of values, and the state is faced with the need either to restructure itself, or destroy the new religion.

This is the historical phenomenon of political conflict because of religious differences.

References

Arcilla, Jose S., S.J. 1978. "The return of the Jesuits in Mindanao." *Philippine Studies* 26:16–34.

———. 1979. "Jessuit missions' policies in the Philippines, 1859–1899." *Philippine Studies* 27:126–97.

———. 1981. *Kinaadman* 3:137–52.

———. 1982. *Kinaadman* 4: 203–57.

Colin, Francisco. 1900. *Labor evangelica*, ed. Pablo Pastells, S.J. Barcelona.

de la Costa, Horacio. 1961. *Jesuits in the Philippines.* Howard University Press.

de Morga, Antonio. 1909. *Sucesos de las Islas Filipinas*. Madrid

Dictionaire de Théoligi Catholique. ---- . 2364–91.

Dunne, George II, S.J. 1962. *A generation of giants*. Notre Dame, Ind.

Porra Camuñez, Jose Luis. 1908. *Sinodo de Manila de 1582.* Madrid.

Retana, Wenceslao E. 1908. *La primera conspiracion de separatista*. Madrid.

Rodriguez, Esteban. 1886. *Coleccion de documentos inéditos*. 2a serie. Madrid.

Rouleau, Francis A, S.J. 1962. "Maillard de Tournon, papal legate at the court of Peking." *Archivum Historicum Societatis Jesu* 31:264–323.

Streit-Dindinger. 1936. *Bibliografica Missionaria*. Romae.

India-Pakistan War Over Kashmir: Terrorism or Legacy of British Divide-and-rule Policy?

Benito O. Lim

Everyone talks about terror—but no one has defined the act to everyone's satisfaction. Neither UN Resolutions nor NATO documents that condemn terrorism come close to informing us what it is. The Russians, however, are clear as to who the terrorists are: they are the Chechens who are fighting for independence. The Chinese are also clear about who they are: They are the Sinkiang Muslim separatists and the followers of the Dalai Lama. Even Ariel Sharon is clear—they are Arafat and the Palestinians. And of course, to the Palestinians, they are Ariel Sharon and the Israelis.

The status of the terrorists also changes from day to day. Yesterday Menachem Begin and Nelson Mandela were called "terrorists." Today they are the winners of the Nobel Peace Prize. Yesterday Yasser Arafat won the Nobel Peace Prize. Osama bin Laden and al-Qaeda were the CIA's "freedom fighters." Today they are the most fearsome of terrorists. In our new century, terrorist or terrorism appears to be temporary appellations. Nobody can be a permanent terrorist.

Definitions of terrorism are too broad while others are too narrow. Here are two examples. Pres. George W. Bush's Executive Order of June 27, 2001 ordering the freezing and blocking of donations to a list of persons "engaged in or supporting extremist violence" is a narrow definition. President Bush said that extremist violence "constitutes an unusual and extraordinary threat to the national security and foreign policy of the U.S., and hereby declares a national emergency to deal with that threat."

Clearly anybody who threatens U.S. security and foreign policy is a terrorist. Anybody or any organization in the U.S. list of terrorists is a terrorist. Indeed much of what is said and done by the U.S. government derives from and is justified by this arbitrary appraisal.

In contrast, a November 2000 report of the UN Sixth Committee defines terrorism in these general terms: "Criminal acts intended or calculated to provoke a state of terror to the general public, a group of persons or particular persons for political reasons are in any circumstances unjustifiable, whatever the considerations of a political, philosophical, ideological, racial, ethnic, religious, or other nature that may be used to justify them."

This definition is so broad that any act that provokes a state of terror is terrorism and unjustifiable by whatever principle or cause. Hasn't the U.S. provoked a state of terror among groups of innocent Afghanistan civilians who migrated by the millions to Pakistan when it bombed Afghanistan? Indeed during the American and British bombing of Afghanistan, countless innocent civilians were killed. These acts, by the above definition, are unjustifiable under any circumstances and whatever the considerations.

Fortunately our own Sen. Rodolfo Biazon and parliamentarians from twenty-six countries in Asia and Pacific rejected the U.S. unilateral definition of terrorism and instead are urging the UN to come out with a universally accepted definition.

The UN accordingly has avoided any clear-cut definition since some parts of the definition may contradict one of the charter's principles: the right of self-determination. There are, of course, people who believe that political violence or terrorism can sometimes legitimately be used to correct social or political injustices (Lacquer 1987).[1]

The question I raise in this essay on the fifty-five-year off-and-on India-Pakistan War over Kashmir is whether the killings, maiming, destruction of property, and dislocation of large populations by bombings, small and large wars, and kidnappings, are justifiable acts to address unresolved historical issues. Or whether they

1 For more detailed and systematic discussion on terrorism, see also Rubenstein, 1987; McForan 1988.

are the outcome of deliberate colonial policy of divide and rule or a matter of territorial conflict or a war of civilizations or the pursuit of self-determination, or cases of state terrorism and suppression. Answers may depend on which side you belong. The Indians and Pakistanis do not engage in a German-style of soul-searching that took place after World War II. According to the Indian historian Gyanendra Pandey, "Indian intellectuals have tended to celebrate the story of the Independence struggle than dwell on the agonies of Partition."

Yet as we follow conflict from the period of British rule, to Partition, to independence to the call for self-determination by the Kashmiris, it will be to no one's surprise that it is a compound of all these factors. If we examined the violence and brutalities the Hindus, Sikhs, and Muslims inflicted against one another, they fit any general definition of terrorism—over two and a half million lives were lost, about two million of whom were those of innocent men, women, and children.

The British Raj and the Hindu-Muslim Divide

Contemporary Indian and Pakistani leaders tend to blame the British divide-and-rule policies, particularly the partition of the subcontinent into two states, for the off-and-on fifty-five-year old India-Pakistan War. British historians, however, claim that communal repression between Hindus and Muslims dates back centuries before the British colonization of India. It can be traced to the practice of Muslim conquerors who rode down through the Khyber Pass and forced their conquered Hindu subjects to convert into Islam. Many Indian political scientists, like Ashis Nandy, agree that the communal tension has long historical roots. But many contemporary political analysts also contend that much of Hindu-Muslim antagonism started only after the arrival of the British and the rise of modern nationalist ideologies. Large-scale persecution of religious minorities that took place in Medieval Europe was unknown in India despite Akbar's Moghul Empire, Bijapur under the Adil Shahi dynasty, and Zainal Abidin's rule of Kashmir (Mishra 2001). During these early years, the peoples of South Asia tended to define themselves in terms of their family allegiances, caste, linguistic group, and not in political categories as Hindus and Muslims. "Hinduism" in fact is a category invented by the British in the nineteenth century to refer to the civilization of the people living beyond the river of Indus. It was later used by Hindu nationalists to unite the largest ethnic group in India, but tended to overlook the historical heritage of India which included Muslims from Persia and Central Asia and their descendants for much of the last eight centuries. "India was once a part of the Moghul Empire of the sixteenth and seventeenth centuries, the center of the Islamic world" (ibid.).

This Hindu bias has its origins in the early self-serving accounts of British historians of India who invariably described the Hindus as "backward," "indolent," and "apathetic," while the Muslims were pictured as "ruthless tyrants" and "religious fanatics."

The British Raj, however, exploited this historical antagonism to maintain its rule in India. The British Raj not only exacerbated but also entrenched communal barriers. And as one British scholar wrote: "They divided, we unified them and ruled. "

To Anita Desai, "the idea of a single, unified nation" was not a British legacy. "It was the dream of every invader who entered India through its high mountain passes on horseback and with sword in hand, from the eighth century onward, inflamed by passion to conquer the whole land" (Desai 1997). After conquest, however, there was relative absence of Hindu-Muslim violence.

To many other political leaders the primary issue before the grant of independence to the subcontinent was not whether to divide the Indian subcontinent into "two nations" (MacFarquhar 1997), but the manner and speed with which the British implemented the Partition. Much was known about the diverse religious sects, castes, folk and elite cultures, philosophies, traditions, and language that have existed and that led to communal conflicts. A more systematic approach to partition could have prevented the pointless killing of thousands of lives. By the early-twentieth century many Hindus and the Muslims were already convinced "that each deserved its own homeland," but violence could have been averted if culture, religion, and language were factored in as guidelines to the partition of the Indian subcontinent.

Nineteenth-century British emphasis on Hindu-Muslim separateness led people like the philosopher Mohammad Iqbal, a Kashmiri, one of the first Muslim leaders, to advance the idea of a separate homeland for the Muslims. Iqbal observed that the Muslims under the British Raj were being systematically marginalized. Islam weakened when it mingled with the local traditions of Hinduism. For this reason, its purity could not be advanced in a country dominated by Hindus. True Islam can only be preserved if Indian Muslims formed a separate nation (Khan 1997). There was also the Muslim fear that in the twentieth century the Hindus would be forced to subordinate their religion, culture, economics, and politics to Hindu majority rule (Pandey in Guha 1997).

Contemporary Origins of Hindu-Muslim Divide

To most Indian scholars, the British should have presented a blueprint for the two states and a map of the component states to the Indian National Congress years before the Partition. At that time both Jawarharlal Nehru and M. A. Jinnah were loyal members of the Congress. As it turned out, Lord Mountbatten, the last viceroy of India, not only showed obvious bias in favor of Nehru and his Congress Party, but also ordered Sir Cyril Radcliffe, the supposedly neutral Boundary commissioner, to make critical map adjustments in favor of India (Sengupta 1997).

To many other political analysts, it was Jawaharlal Nehru's refusal to share power with Muslim leaders that made inevitable the partition of India (Frank 2001). In June 1946, Nehru told a press conference that the central government of an independent India would reserve its rights to intervene in the component states of the union on issue of planning and economic development (MacFarquhar 1997). Jinnah, the founder of Pakistan, viewed Nehru's statement as treachery. According to Sengupta's account, at crucial moments in India's transition to independence in 1947, Nehru exerted influence over Lord Mountbatten to keep Kashmir and its Muslim majority as part of India. Nehru, a self-confessed agnostic, was convinced that the idea of separate nations for the Muslims, the "two-nation theory," first proposed by Mohammad Iqbal, was a mistake. In appreciation of Mountbatten's favor, Nehru kept India within the Commonwealth even when India was already a republic. This has led other former British colonies to follow Nehru's example.

Many Indian intellectuals who had access to Western-style education supported Nehru's position. Nehru did not want to define India in specifically Hindu terms but as a confluence of many cultures and religions. These intellectuals claimed that even after Partition, India is still the third largest Muslim nation in the world (Sen 1997). The best way to unite the nation is to give the Muslims access to Western-style education. Indian intellectuals were convinced that it was Western-style education that created "a pan-Indian intelligentsia"—and produced people like Gandhi, Nehru, and Tagore. Unfortunately "the Muslims of India were late to embrace Western-style education that provided the Hindus access to new ideas" (Mishra 2000). According to Rabindranath Tagore, a Hindu Nobel laureate, compared to the Muslims, the Hindus were lucky because "circumstances almost compel us to learn English, and this lucky accident has given us the opportunity of access into the richest of all poetical literatures of the world." Tagore made a distinction between the injustice of a series asymmetry of power (colonialism) and the importance, nevertheless, of Western culture. In parts of India and in what is now known as Bangladesh, many Muslims shared a deep sense with Tagore about the importance of Western-style education. They even adopted one of Tagore's songs, "Amar Sonar Bangla" (My Golden Bengal) as their national anthem (Sen 1997).

Whether Western education would have liberated the Muslim mind and therefore suppress their desire for a separate nation is a debatable matter. But scholars on the subject say that it is sufficient to note that when the educated Muslims sensed that independence was a possibility in the early-twentieth century, they worried about Hindu dominance in Indian politics. The agitation and campaign for two nations became more intense. Indian Muslims rejected the outlook of Hindu liberals of building an India in the image of Britain.

Consequences of British Partition of India and Pakistan

What came to be known as the period of Partition was a time when local wars between the Hindus and Muslims became more violent. In the account of Roderick MacFarquhar, "on the plains of Punjab, the proudest province of British India, which had just been partitioned between the successor states, India and Pakistan, was collapsing into a state of nature. Sikhs and Hindus killed their Muslim neighbors; Muslims killed Sikhs and Hindus. Millions of Hindus and Sikhs fled eastward to India, Muslims westward to Pakistan. Hundreds of thousands did not make it" (Banga in MacFarquhar 1997).

Later accounts of "ethnic cleansing" during Partition revealed that refugees who tried to leave for India or Pakistan were massacred before they reached either border (Burke and Quaraishi 1995, 342–56). The number of dead as a result of Partition ranged from one million to two million.[2] People writing about this period were shocked by brutal murders of innocent civilians, especially of women and children, and condemned the senseless violence.

Hindu, Muslim and Sikh soldiers who composed the proud British Indian Army had divided themselves into the armed forces of the new nations. They were poised to destroy one another in the province of Kashmir, which is located between India and Pakistan, and which suffered one of the largest number of casualties (Jha 1996).[3]

Nehru and the Accession of Kashmir

MacFarquhar noted that as a consequence of Nehru's lobby with Mountbatten, Kashmir was not made part of Pakistan. As early as the 1940s about 90 percent of the people living in Kashmir were Muslims, and only 5 percent were Hindus and the rest were Sikhs. The decision to join India or Pakistan was left to the maharajah.

The maharajah, a Hindu, ruled the largest state under British paramountcy. A year before Partition, the maharajah lobbied that Kashmir should not be a part of Pakistan. He even ordered his Hindu Army to crack down on Muslim activists who wanted to join Pakistan outright. One of the Muslim leaders he imprisoned was Sheikh Abdullah, a brilliant follower of Iqbal and was known as "the Lion of Kashmir." Abdullah started his career as a fighter for India's independence and became the most popular leader of Kashmiri Muslims. Abdullah became a close associate of Nehru during their campaign

2 Larry Collins and Dominique Lapierre, Freed at Midnight (Simon and Schuster, 1975) quoted estimates from 200 thousand to 500 thousand.Later estimates with more comprehensive data ranged from 1 to 2 million dead. See Patrick French 1997.

3 See also Ahmed 1997.

for independence. Nehru confided to Abdullah that his ancestors came from Kashmir, and his father moved to Delhi and Allahabad in 1889 to start his law practice (Nehru 1980). Nehru told Abdullah that though his body was confined to India his soul "existed in Kashmir."

Indeed their close association during the campaign for independence had convinced Nehru that Abdullah shared his conviction that "the old social economic order of India, represented by the maharajahs and big landlords, had to be destroyed through land reforms and centralized economic planning" (Mishra 2000, 33). Nehru told Abdullah to rally both the Hindu majority in Jammu and the small minorities in the Kashmir Valley to turn against the maharajah. Sticking to the Muslims alone was not going to win the cooperation of the other sectors of Kashmir.

On learning that Nehru was supporting a Muslim leader in Kashmir, the maharajah, for self-preservation, became receptive to emissaries from Pakistan. Over the next months, he listened to what the Pakistani emissaries had to offer him.

Unfortunately for the maharajah, in the latter months after Partition, violence and rioting had led Sikhs from Pakistan to join his Hindu Army in attacking Muslims in Kashmir. Tens of thousands of Muslims were killed. Many fled to Pakistan, where news of the killings outraged the Muslims in the Pakistan border. As an act of vengeance, a handful of Pakistan Muslim officers rallied some of the Muslim tribes in the border and waged a jihad against the maharajah. The maharajah's Army was easily routed. But the attack outraged Pakistan's central government, which was still trying to win over the maharajah to join Kashmir with Pakistan (ibid., 34).

Believing that he was betrayed the maharajah immediately appealed to India for military assistance. Nehru delayed sending his Army into Kashmir. He told the maharajah that the Indian Army could enter Kashmir only after Kashmir formally acceded to India. Fearful that he might be captured by the Pakistani jihadis (Islamic warriors), the maharajah agreed to sign a formal accession and never returned to Kashmir. He remained in Bombay till his death. His son, Karan Singh, faithfully recorded the events leading to the formal accession (Singh 1989).

The Indian Army entered Srinagar, capital of Kashmir, in October 1947 and waged against Pakistan a full-scale war, which lasted for over a year (Schofield 2000).

Despite the war, Pakistan refused to recognize Kashmir's accession to India. As far as the Pakistanis were concerned the maharajah was blackmailed and tricked into accession. Moreover there was no nationwide referendum, therefore, accession was not legal. This led Nehru on January 1, 1948 to appeal to the UN to conduct a plebiscite to confirm the accession. But the plebiscite did not take place. The UN, however, brokered a ceasefire on 1 January 1949. A line of control (LOC) divided Kashmir into two sides. The LOC is now regarded as a de facto international border. The northwestern part closer to the Muslim Punjab, or a third of the real estate, remained under Pakistan control while Srinagar, Jammu, and Kashmir Valley, or two-thirds of Kashmir, remained under Indian control. Both India and Pakistan and Kashmir from 1948 to 1953 accepted the LOC.

Ironically it was Abdullah, released from prison a few weeks before the invasion, who organized the defense of Kashmir against the invading pro-Pakistani guerrillas. His defense of Kashmir and Kashmir's accession led Nehru to appoint Abdullah as the prime minister of Kashmir. His plan now was to strengthen India's control by sharing political power with Abdullah. Unfortunately for Nehru, Kashmir saw through his plan. As a consequence the relationship between Nehru and Abdullah remained to be an alliance of convenience. The alliance was put to test in 1949 when Abdullah started a series of land reforms, whereby lands of big Hindu landlords were taken away and distributed to poor Muslim tenants. The Hindus of Jammu charged that Abdullah was biased in favor of the Kashmiri Muslims and against the Hindus of Kashmir. Many Hindu leaders of Jammu wanted Abdullah removed as prime minister. The radical Hindus of the Congress party agreed. Abdullah pleaded with Nehru to allow him to continue his land reform program by making Kashmir autonomous, free from the politics of the Congress party, but Nehru turned down Abdullah's proposal. Yet years earlier, it was Nehru who persuaded Abdullah to pursue economic policies based on socialist lines. Over the next months Abdullah decided to revive his idea of an independent Kashmir. He even discussed the idea with

U.S. Ambassador Adlai Stevenson who visited Kashmir in 1953 (Mishra 2000).

When Nehru was told about Abdullah's plan to work for an independent Kashmir, he acted immediately. He dismissed Abdullah as prime minister and jailed him without trial. Abdullah languished in jail for eleven years. Nehru explained to the international press that Abdullah was working against India's "national interest." In truth Nehru feared losing Kashmir. He told his people that Kashmir could not be separated from India without giving separatist ideas to other Muslims in the rest of India. And as soon as Kashmir became independent, there would be nationwide communal riots by the Muslims (Gopal 1980). Nehru insisted on intervening in Kashmiri politics because he believed that the Muslim majority in Kashmir wanted independence. When Abdullah was imprisoned the Muslims in Kashmir were convinced that Nehru had no intention of turning all Hindus and Muslims into equal citizens of a secular and democratic nation-state. Rather Nehru only wanted to reduce the Muslims to a perpetually powerless minority in an India ruled by the Hindu-dominated Congress.

Abdullah remained in prison even after Nehru's death in 1964. He was released in 1975. He was made chief minister of the state on condition that he give up his demand for independence. Disillusioned nationalists said he became a willing satrap of the Indian state in Kashmir.[4] Some called him the "Toothless Lion of Kashmir," whose dentures bore the imprint of Indira Gandhi. Many knowledgeable Kashmiris with no cause to admire Abdullah felt that Kashmir's accession to India resulted in less political freedom, not more. For a time when the Kashmiris fought the invading pro-Pakistani guerrillas it seemed that the Indian government was willing to grant the promise that accession would go hand in hand with freedom.

A few months before Abdullah died, he appointed his son Farooq Abdullah, a practicing doctor of medicine from London, as his successor. Farooq was reputed to be more independent than his father. But his leadership was short-lived. When Farooq refused to accept Prime Minister Indira Gandhi's offer of an election alliance

4 After 1965, the head Kashmir was no longer referred to as prime minister but, as in other Indian states, as chief minister.

between her Congress Party and his National Conference Party in 1983, she was determined to get rid of him. She attributed any anti-India demonstration in Kashmir, big or small, to Farooq's handiwork. The Indian press repeated Indira's charges. The enemies of India, when they were not CIA minions or Pakistan-trained rebels, were Farooq's Muslims from Kashmir or rebellious Sikhs. To reduce the power of Farooq, Indira appointed Jagmohan, a Hindu leader from Jammu as governor of Jammu and Kashmir. In early 1984, before her assassination, she engineered in Kashmir, through bribes paid to legislators, the collapse of a democratically elected government. It was the first of a series of events that forced Kashmiri Muslims into a full-scale anti-India insurgency in the 1990s. Mrs. Gandhi insisted in early 1984 that the Sikhs and Kashmiri Muslims were threats to India's "unity and integrity." In short, however important the earlier cooperation and collaboration of the Sikhs and Muslims were in her political campaign to win over a majority for her Congress Party, they remained insignificant in her overall scheme of things. As it turned out they occupied a most ambiguous place, and thus were politically and ideologically suspect.

Muslim Rebellion in the State of Kashmir

After Indira's Sikh bodyguards assassinated her in October, Jagmohan illegally dismissed Farooq's elected government. Between the eighties and early nineties he, more than "anyone else," did more "to provoke insurgency in the state of Kashmir. In the mid-eighties, he sought to impose "a peculiarly Hindu modernity on the state of Kashmir." He allowed unrestricted sale of alcohol but prohibited the slaughter of sheep on a Hindu festival day. Jagmohan charged that Muslims were dirtying Hindu communities by slaughtering cows in their slaughter houses. Muslims were drug pushers who convinced Hindu maidens to elope. The number of Muslims in government service went down. He encouraged the migration of non-Muslims into Muslim areas. The backlash came almost immediately. "The popularity of Islamist parties grew and grew all through the 1980s, helped by the growth of *madrasas* (Muslim theology schools)... often run by Muslims from Assam in eastern India, over a thousand miles away, where mass killings of Muslims in the early eighties had forced their migration to Kashmir" (Mishra 2000, 36). In 1987 even the popular Farooq who teamed up with the Congress Party would have lost the election to Syed Salahudin, leader of Hizbul Mujahideen, had Indian police and military not intervened. Candidates and polling agents of Islamist parties were beaten up and tortured. Salahudin himself was imprisoned after having nearly won the race.

No doubt, during the brief term of Rajiv Gandhi, Indira's elder son, between 1985 and 1989, the Indian economy improved dramatically. Commercialism bloomed in India, and a new entrepreneurial middle class emerged—the small shopkeepers and petty traders became more aggressive, unscrupulous, and richer. The poor from rural India moved into the cities for a share of the new wealth. Unfortunately millions from the neglected provinces like Kashmir found themselves held back for lack of an education, technology, economic wealth, or out of the restriction placed on them by the ancient tradition of caste and religion. Resentment in the neglected and forgotten provinces swelled even as the cities prospered, skyscrapers rose higher, and downtown streets crowded with cars of all makes and sizes.

Those left outside the orbit of prosperity became more resentful, and in Kashmir large numbers of young people, disillusioned by Indian misrule and oversight, seething with bitterness, traveled to Pakistan either to pursue higher education or to receive training as jihadis.There was the widespread belief that a new political order or an independent Kashmir was the essential prerequisite for the economic rehabilitation and growth of the state. In their view Kashmir has been neglected by India. It remains one of the most backward and impoverished regions. The tiny and preponderantly Hindu-dominated industries have been so ravaged by more than four decades of guerrilla war, bombings, banditry, kidnapping, ambuscades, police and army "crackdowns." Kashmir's inadequate system of transportation and communication lay in shambles. The population provided with a minimum level of existence during the best of times, faced food shortages and famine from time to time. Agriculture in Kashmir was still at the stage it was centuries ago. The contrast of their lives with the more cosmopolitan parts of India was more stark and shocking, for they still lived in encampments of shacks with little water, health care, schools, or even food. What was new in the mid-eighties was the rage of the have-nots, whose manners were increasingly brusque and speeches vehement and defiant, threatening to wage a revolution in Kashmir.

The young Kashmiris who went to Afghanistan and Pakistan were trained for months in guerrilla warfare and the use of weapons, and given salaries as well as free private housing. Others became gunrunners bringing arms and munitions into the Kashmir Valley. From 1986 thereon the thousands of young Kashmiris were organized by the CIA through Pakistan's International Services Intelligence (ISI) and Bin Laden's al-Qaeda, into guerrilla groups that went to Afghanistan to fight the Soviet-supported regime. But others went back to Kashmir and began a war of liberation in 1990 (Puri 1995).

Kashmir Muslim Connection with Pakistan, U.S. CIA and Osama bin Laden

In 1979 when the Soviet Union invaded Afghanistan, Pakistan became America's base of operation. The CIA found Pakistan a ready and willing host for its proxy war against the Soviet Union. For ten years, the CIA poured into Pakistan billions of dollars worth of arms and ammunition. This turned its office in Islamabad into the largest CIA operating center next to its main office in Langley, Virginia. The arms were supposed to be given to the *mujahideen* fighting the Soviet Army in Afghanistan, and to finance the illegal drug trade. The drug project turned out to be counterproductive. Apart from creating five million addicts in Pakistan, the heroin traders were able to link up with drug distributors in New York.

By the early 1980s, William Casey, CIA director under Pres. Ronald Reagan, conceived of an international Muslim group to fight the Soviet Union. He asked the Pakistani intelligence, or the Inter-Service Intelligence (ISI), and Abdullah Azzam, founder of the Makhtab al-Khimat, or Service Center, to organize a global jihad center against the Soviet Union. Muslim recruits from all over the world would be given military training, arms, as well as money. Casey's idea of an international jihadi group appealed to many Muslim leaders in the Middle East. Saudi Arabia and many other American allies contributed money for this effort. It was during this period when young Muslims from Kashmir, refugees numbering to three million from Afghanistan and another forty thousand volunteers from Chechnya, Malaysia, Indonesia, the Philippines, and China went to Pakistan and Afghanistan for training. Parenthetically this was the period when some of members of the MNLF, MILF, and Abu Sayyaf from the Philippines joined the CIA-sponsored training program.

It was during this period, too, when the name Osama bin Laden surfaced as a household name to young and idealistic Muslim jihadis.

Osama bin Laden of Saudi Arabia is the son of a Yemen-born construction tycoon in Saudi Arabia, one of fifty-three children and the seventeenth son of the twelfth wife and his mother's only child.[5] His father owned one of the largest construction companies in Saudi Arabia, that had the sole contract for the repair and renovation of the holy Islamic sites at Mecca and Medina.As a child, he played with sons of Saudi princes and child-dignitaries. His father has been an influential donor not only within the Saudi kingdom but also in Europe and America. In the early nineties, his father established two fellowships in Islamic studies at Harvard University. One of his brothers, who works at Harvard, denounces and disowns him as a relative.

His family's headquarters in Jeddah, used to receive high-profile guests such as the former Pres. George H. W. Bush, father of George W., and James Baker. No doubt, the Bin Ladens, in addition to being close to great powers in the kingdom, are well connected with the powers of the Western world. This pedigree is not mere background information; it is central to the life of Osama bin Laden and his later notoriety.

In 1979 during the Soviet invasion of Afghanistan, Bin Laden had just obtained a civil engineering degree at the King Abdul Aziz University in Jeddah, Saudi Arabia. According to one account, he was one of the graduates invited by Prince Turki Faisal, head of Saudi intelligence, to raise funds across Saudi Arabia and other Gulf States to advance the cause of Wahhabism, Saudi's version of Islamic Fundamentalism. He turned out to be an efficient fund raiser and

5 For a more exhaustive account of Bin Laden see Bodansky 2002 and Reeve 2002.

a good businessman. His inheritance of $50 million ballooned into $300 million. But it was only in 1984 when he finally moved his own construction company into Pakistan and Afghanistan. While in Pakistan, he was persuaded by Prince Turki to join the anti-Communist jihad and to help mobilize the foreign volunteers. Some biographers claim that he was Prince Turki's gift to William Casey, CIA director under Pres. Ronald Reagan.

Bin Laden met Abdullah Azzam, who was a professor at King Abdul Aziz University and who broke with the PLO's Hamas on the grounds that it was not fundamental enough. Azzam instead founded the worldwide network of Muslim militants, Makhtab al-Khimat, or Service Center, when the Soviet Union invaded Afghanistan. In the 1980s, with the CIA's blessings, he set up fund-raising organizations in the United States from Brooklyn to Detroit to Los Angeles. Their network also received money from Muslims the world over which they used to put up foundations all over the world. They gave the money to Muslim volunteers and their families. As the distributor of the Saudi money, which matched dollar for dollar the American assistance to the jihad against the Soviet regime in Afghanistan, Bin Laden became a very famous man in Pakistan and Afghanistan. William Casey dubbed the members of Makhtab al-Khimat, later known as al-Qaeda, as "freedom fighters." Al-Qaeda recruits were given military training and arms, as well as CIA and Saudi money (Yousaf and Adkin 1992).

It was Bin Laden's association with Azzam and during the training of the Islamic jihadis that Bin Laden found his sense of purpose.

When the Russians withdrew from Afghanistan in 1989, Azzam turned his attention to Israeli-occupied territories. A few months later Israel's Mossad assassinated him and his two sons. After Azzam's death, Bin Laden took over Makhtab-al-Khidmat and founded al-Qaeda, or the Base.

During the Gulf War Bin Laden offered his al-Qaeda group to fight Iraq. But the Saudi royal family preferred American troops. This led Bin Laden to attack the Saudi regime as a puppet of the Americans. Due to his unrelenting attacks against the Saudi royal family and the presence of American troops in Saudi Arabia, the Saudi regime stripped Bin Laden of his citizenship in 1994. American and Saudi pressure also forced the Sudanese government to deport Bin Laden. In 1996 he and his four wives and children left Sudan for Jalalabad, a city in Afghanistan. It was in this city where Bin Laden first met the Taliban.

The Taliban at first were suspicious of Bin Laden. They thought he was a spy. But his willingness to spend hundreds of millions of dollars for their conquest of Kabul endeared him to Mullah Mohammad Omar. It was this association that led Bin Laden to spend the next five years formulating his new ideology, as well as recruiting and training his al-Qaeda warriors.

In 1998 he issued his manifesto "The International Islamic Front for Jihad against Jews and Crusaders." The manifesto denounced the U.S. "for occupying the lands of Islam in the holiest of places, the Arabian Peninsula, plundering its riches, dictating to its rulers, humiliating its people, and terrorizing its neighbors." He accused the U.S. of turning Saudi Arabia, Iraq, Egypt and Sudan into "paper statelets" in order to "guarantee Israel's survival." The manifesto enjoined his Islamic jihadis of the world "to kill the Americans and their allies—civilians and military." It continued that killing Americans "is an individual duty for every Muslim who can do it in any country in which it is possible to do it, in order to liberate the al-Aqsa Mosque and the holy mosque (Mecca) from their grip, and in order for their armies to move out of all the lands of Island, defeated and unable to threaten any Muslim." His new ideology led CIA analysts to classify him as an "international terrorist." The CIA listed Osama bin Laden as one of the conspirators in the first bombing of the World Trade Center (WTC) in 1993. For five years one of the main tasks of the CIA's Counter-Terrorism Center (CTC) was to contain the dangers posed by Bin Laden (Powers 2002).

Six months after Bin Laden issued his *fatwa* (manifesto), the U.S. embassies in Kenya and Tanzania were bombed. In November 1998, a Manhattan federal court issued an indictment containing 238 charges of terrorism against Bin Laden covering the 1993 bombing of the WTC to an assassination plot against President Clinton in 1994, and funding of Islamist groups in the U.S. In 1999, the UN Security Council passed a resolution condemning Bin Laden for sponsoring international terrorism. The U.S. government's chief witness was an al-Qaeda defector, Jamal Ahmed al Fadl, who absconded with $110,000 worth of commission from the organization. In his testimony, he said that Bin Laden's al-Qaeda has links with Islamist groups in Algeria, Yemen, Egypt, the Philippines, Chechnya, Indonesia, Malaysia, and other countries with large Islamic populations. Many of the links were either political dissidents or poor Muslims escaping from poverty and the wretched life in their countries.

The international corps of jihadis, which began as CIA warriors against the godless Soviet Union, became Bin Laden's main corps in fighting American imperialism the world over. Indeed many of Bin Laden's jihadis now lead Islamic fundamentalist movements in Egypt, Algeria, and the Central Asian Republics.

The Kashmir Muslim connection with Pakistan went deeper. Pakistan fought two wars with India to liberate Kashmir, first in 1948 and then in 1965. In 1990 as well as in 2002, they almost came close to a nuclear war, when "a group of armed men" opened fire in India's Parliament and killed several Indian legislators. Prime Minister Atal Behari Vajpayee insisted that it was the handiwork of Pakistan-backed terrorists but Pakistan Pres. Peshwar Musharraf strongly denied any involvement.

It is undeniable, however, that many Kashmiri Muslims look toward Pakistan for assistance in their struggle for independence. Indeed Pakistan was the only country that consistently affirmed the Kashmiri "right to self-determination." Numerous Kashmiri Muslims received their education on the fundamentals of the Koran and the *Shariah* from the madrasas in Pakistan. The Pakistan Army has thousands of Islamic fundamentalists in its ranks.

Moreover, large scores of Pakistan Army officers have not only religious but also ethnic and linguistic affinities with the Kashmiris. When the ISI was overflowing with CIA and Saudi money, many Kashmiris were invited to work in the ISI by Pakistani Army officers. In the mid-eighties many Pakistan Army officers sent over a hundred thousand of unemployed men to fight the jihad in Afghanistan and a few thousand to fight in Kashmir (Mishra 2000). The war in Afghanistan gave Pakistan fundamentalists the opportunity to realize their mission of creating not only an Islamic state but also a center, or the capital of, a jihad movement, or holy war against infidels. It also gave Pakistan Muslim Army officers an excuse to send jihadis into the Kashmir Valley.

Campaign of Kashmir Guerrillas against India and Indian Retaliations

In 1989, Pakistan sent guerrillas into Kashmir to undertake kidnappings and bombings. Later that year, they kidnapped the daughter of the home minister of the federal government in Delhi, a native of Kashmir. They exchanged her for five guerrillas. When the guerrillas were released and welcomed by large crowds in Srinagar, Indian police killed all five of them. This led to several demonstrations involving hundreds of thousands of men and women who filled the streets of Srinagar shouting “Azadi, azadi!” [Freedom, freedom!] (ibid.).

It is this need for freedom and the sense that they have no future under India “that educated Kashmiris came to have, along with the realization, hammered into them by repeatedly rigged elections, of their political impotence, that eventually led them to the insurgency in the early 1990s” (ibid.).

Since 1990 almost all guerrillas fighting the Indian Army and Police in the Indian-controlled part of Kashmir have been trained in Pakistan or its base in Afghanistan. There are actually two basic guerrilla outfits, the secular guerrilla faction, and the Islamic guerrilla groups. The secular guerrilla faction has been fighting for independence. They are convinced that Kashmir cannot move into the modern world under conditions of economic backwardness. Nothing is more central to these revolutionaries than the need to develop Kashmir economically in order to eliminate extreme social inequalities and oppressive kinds of political despotism.

The Islamic guerrilla groups, such as Hizbul Mujahideen and Lashkar-e-Toiba, are fighting the integration of the Muslim-dominated valley with Pakistan. Unfortunately for the secular guerrillas, they have long been outnumbered by Pakistan-based guerrillas. As far as the Indian government is concerned, since 1990, it has been fighting a brutal “proxy war” with Pakistan in Kashmir.

The number of attacks, counterattacks, and atrocities by both sides were so high, so brutal and the developments so murky that it is difficult to get at the truth. India tends to blame Pakistan for all the bombings and massacres while Pakistan tends to deny these charges and instead blames India as the author of a great number of these deeds.

The Hindu population in Kashmir Valley has been reduced from half a million to 130 thousand. Majority had migrated to India after Muslim guerrillas killed hundreds among them. There are over four million Muslims in Kashmir.

Fighting in Kashmir, however, was no longer confined to Hindus and Muslims. In March 2000, when Pres. Bill Clinton was on an official visit to India, thirty-five Sikhs were killed in Chitisinghpura, a village in the southeastern part of Kashmir valley. Historically the Sikhs, who formed only 2 percent of the population, were neutral. Since the start of the campaign by Kashmiri Muslims for independence in 1990, the Sikhs have maintained their neutrality. For this reason both the Indian Army and the Muslim guerrillas did not target them. The Indian police, who investigated the event, immediately blamed it on the Islamic guerrillas from Pakistan in spite of lack of evidence (ibid.). Opinion polls conducted by Indian newspapers in English had shown majority of the Indians demanding an "all-out invasion of Pakistan." Letters to the editor called for a nuclear attack on Pakistan. Hundreds of thousands of students took to the streets and denounced Pakistan.

Three days after the killing, while President Clinton was still in India, the Indian police in Delhi announced on TV that the Indian Army had just arrested a man called Yaqub Wagay as one of the killers of the Sikhs. Wagay, accordingly, was identified by the only surviving "foreign mercenaries" caught in an earlier encounter. His five companions were killed. The "encounter" became headline material in most of the Indian newspapers. But thereafter the Indian government found its story about foreign mercenaries contradicted by new evidence. The foreign mercenaries as it turned out were Muslims kidnapped before witnesses by the Indian police. Soon the relatives of the five murdered Muslims were joined by thousands of Muslims demanding justice from the Indian government. The Sikh association in Kashmir no longer insists that the massacre was the handiwork of Muslim jihadis. Some of them talk about possible involvement of Indian security forces (*Kashmir Times*, 28 June 200). When the true circumstance of the murder reached the press, President Clinton had already issued a statement asking Pakistan to rein in the Kashmir guerrillas. Clinton, however, refused to join India in blaming Pakistan for the recent killings in Pakistan. But Clinton also recommended that the two countries resolve their differences.

Pakistani political analysts called attention to the fact that since Clinton left, there has been no further attacks on the Sikhs. They asked why Pakistan-backed guerrillas would want to invite international condemnation with an attack hours before President Clinton's arrival to India. In their view the Indian government in Delhi used this incident and other subsequent massacres to send close to half a million soldiers to Kashmir to suppress the Islamic jihadis. The Union Law minister asked the opposition in the Indian Parliament to drop the plan for an independent investigation into the March and August massacres since it will only make Pakistan "point accusing fingers at India" (*Asian Age*, 9 Aug. 2000).

In another unexplained incident in August 2000, unidentified gunmen massacred over a hundred Hindus, a week after the biggest pro-Pakistan guerrilla outfit, Hizbul Mujahideen, declared a cease-fire. Again the Indian government attributed the massacre to Islamic jihadis working "at the behest of Pakistan." The Indian government explained that the objective of the killings was to destroy the peace process. Other observers were convinced that it was not the Pakistan-supported guerrillas but outfits opposed to the cease-fire that undertook the massacre. Why would Hizbul Mujahideen, they asked, want to cancel its own moves when world attention at the time was focused on the killings in Kashmir?

The Indian Prime Minister Atal Bihari Vajpayee, later, presented these massacres to President Clinton as the reason why he could not negotiate with Pakistan's General Musharraf. There is no doubt that the Indian government has, from the very start, refused to include Pakistan in any cease-fire talks because it considers the problems in Kashmir as an internal matter. From Vajpayee's perspective, India for over half a century has managed to quell internal rebellions and secessionist uprisings in Kashmir without external help. More importantly, it has crushed fundamentalist groups seeking to integrate Kashmir into Pakistan. Indeed more than thirty thousand people, mostly Muslims, were killed, maimed, or have disappeared in the Indian campaign during the last ten years. The Indian Army and police have lost a few thousand men during the same period. Moreover, bitter conflicts between Hindus and Muslims continue in many parts of India today. Any sign of weakness on the part of government run the real danger of restarting local religious wars that took place in the days of Partition.

There is no doubt that India, during Clinton's visit, was using the massacres of Hindus and Sikhs in Kashmir as a tactic to elicit the basic fear and distrust in the West of anything related to Islamic extremism and, above all, to convince the State Department to put Pakistan as well as the secular Jammu and Kashmir Liberation Front on its list of terrorist states.

9/11 and the Reaffirmation of U.S.-Pakistan Alliance

Before the September 11 attack on America, the U.S. State Department had already embarked on a cautiously pro-India stance. Compared to Pakistan, India is more stable, economically stronger, would not only be a good ally but has a larger market for American goods. There is also the felt sentiment that the Muslims in Pakistan do not approve of Americans. Indeed a Gallup survey after September 11 in Pakistan showed that 83 percent of Pakistanis sympathize with the Taliban and not the U.S. and 82 percent consider Osama bin Laden a holy warrior, not a terrorist. Many Pakistani generals still blame America for the mess in Afghanistan. In India itself many Hindu nationalists in Parliament have said that India has for a long time selected the wrong and losing side in the Cold War. It is about time India turned to the U.S. in order to build a strong military and economic relationship.

Indeed in 1999 Prime Minister Tony Blair suspended Pakistan from the Commonwealth and most European Union members expressed concern for Pakistan's democracy after General Musharraf seized power from Nawaz Sharif, the former prime minister.

Fortunately for Pervez Musharraf, the September 11 attack on the World Trade Center and Pentagon tilted the U.S. once again to Pakistan's side. Pervez Musharraf not only agreed to provide moral and logistical support, intelligence, Pakistan air space and airfield for allied aircraft but also turned against the Taliban. For most political analysts, Musharraf had taken a risky gamble. For as late as 1999 after his successful coup, he and his generals continued to plead the Taliban's case internationally. Musharraf's government continued to give aid to the Taliban government and invited its representatives to Islamabad (de Bellaigue 2001).

In a nationally televised speech, Musharraf explained to his people why he sided with the U.S. It was a choice between "two adversities" and he decided, as prescribed by Islamic law, to take the lesser one. He said that alliance with the U.S. would preserve Pakistan's nuclear program, and allow it to pursue the long-standing desire to secure the Indian-held part of Kashmir and develop the economy with US aid (Rashid 2002).

The lesser adversity also led him to freeze bank accounts of four Islamist organizations that have links with al-Qaeda. Musharraf also turned over records that according to U.S. prosecutors would be sufficient to convict him in court.

Bush lifted sanctions that were imposed when Musharraf suspended democracy in Pakistan. Much of Pakistan's foreign debts were forgiven while others were rescheduled. Several hundred million dollars were released so the general could feed the hundreds of thousands of refugees fleeing Afghanistan and moving into Pakistan borders. Even the sanctions imposed in 1998, when Pakistan following India's example detonated its nuclear weapons, were lifted.[6]

More importantly, Musharraf's international image has been changed from that of a terrorist to a freedom fighter. Prime Minister Tony Blair had to travel all the way to Islamabad to congratulate him for his "courage and leadership." By praising him, Blair has said, in effect, that he was sorry for keeping Pakistan out of the Commonwealth.Western human rights advocates, who predicted that Musharraf had no chance of surviving the anger of his Muslim constituents, said in October 2001 that he would win the elections hands down. And he did. But they are not so certain that he could survive the challenge from India.

6 For a more exhaustive discussion in nuclear weapons see Ramana and Nayyar 2001.

Domestically most Pakistanis are tired of the Kashmir issue, and would prefer that the government spend the money on education, infrastructure, and delivery of health services rather than on military campaigns against India. Unfortunately the Pakistani military leadership has a different view.

Terrorism and Response

On December 13, 2001, a group of armed men opened fire in India's Parliament, killing fourteen people in an unprecedented attack on the seat of government. Prime Minister Atal Vajpayee immediately blamed the Pakistani Army for complicity, after a Pakistan-based militant group claimed responsibility for the attack. Hawks within the ruling Bharatiya Janata Party (BJP) asked for immediate military reprisal for the attack. They charged that Pakistan was engaged in state terrorism. Pakistan strongly denied the charge. And immediately both sides massed over a million soldiers along the 2,912-kilometer Kashmir frontier and launched artillery gunfire at each other. But political observers were apprehensive that the border showdown might escalate into a full-scale nuclear war. Both sides detonated nuclear devices as late as 1999.

Under pressure from Pres. George W. Bush, the foreign ministers of both countries prepared for a meeting in Katmandu. On January 4, Prime Minister Vajpayee and President Musharraf met, shook hands, marking the first time they had met face to face. According to Vajpayee they had "courtesy talks," but no serious dialogue. They shook hands again on Sunday and parted company. Musharraf told reporters in a news conference that tensions "may not have been eased, but haven't worsened" (Reuters 2002).

Their failure to dialogue prompted President Bush to send Sec. of State Colin Powell to persuade the two heads of state to meet and "find a solution to the situation." He managed to obtain a promise from President Musharraf to crack down on the "Islamic extremists" in Pakistan.

While arrangements were being made for the heads of state to meet, bombings by domestic "extremists" were going on both in Pakistan and India. There was renewed fighting between Hindus and Muslims in India's Ahmedabad, Gujarat, Bapunagar, Gomtipur,

Kadhi, and Pradesh. There were also attacks on American religious centers in both countries.

In June 2002 at an Asian security summit, India and Pakistan continued to blame each other for the fifty-five years of conflict over Kashmir. President Musharraf said within the hearing distance of Prime Minister Vajpayee, “We do not want war. If war is imposed on us, we will defend ourselves with the utmost resolution...The people of South Asia continue to pay a heavy price for the refusal by India to resolve the Kashmir dispute in accordance with resolutions of the UN and the wishes of the Kashmiri people” (Associated Press 2002).

Vajpayee in turn accused Pakistan of trying to use nuclear blackmail and rejected Musharraf’s repeated assurance that Pakistan will not allow its territory to be used for any terrorist attacks outside or inside its boundaries. Vajpayee said: “We have seen in the following months that cross-border infiltration has increased, violence in Jammu and Kashmir has continued unabated and terrorist camps continue to exist across our border. We have repeatedly said that we are willing to discuss all issues with Pakistan, including Jammu and Kashmir. But for that, cross-border terrorism has to end” (ibid.).

Kashmir Independence Likely Solution to End India-Pakistan Conflict

And so after fifty-five years, two major wars, ten years of proxy war, there is still a nuclear war looming in the background. A costly arms race continues, more lethal nuclear weapons are being developed, missiles are deployed against each other, over a million soldiers are still shooting at one another at the Kashmiri border, and small wars and ambushes are going on unabated. What is the war over Kashmir all about?

Kashmiri old-timers and historians say that there is nothing new about their circumstances. As far as they can remember and recalling the tales of their parents and grandparents, Kashmir was largely agrarian for hundreds of years. It remains so under Indian rule of fifty-five years. In addition, Kashmir has chronic problems of unemployment and underemployment, inefficient local administration, a population preyed upon by gangsters, widespread drug addiction, prostitution, and lack of elemental standards of sanitation and municipal services. Kashmir today faces more acute problems than when it was under the British Raj. Under Indian rule, politicians buy votes from citizens, businessmen buy favors and licenses from politicians and bureaucrats. Citizens pay "facilitation or service fees" to the police and petty officials for access to services. Of course, Kashmiri historians concede that under the Moguls, Afghani, and Sikh invaders, the peasantry was also taxed into absolute misery.

But few people, the old-timers observed, unless they lived in Kashmir for a while, will notice the wretchedness of the poor. The physical splendor and beauty of the place usually overwhelm them. Tourists are shown streams of cool, clear water that divide villages, the meadowed bank with bathing cabin of rough timber and the leafless willows and the grazing stray cow. Or taken to ride in tiny boats becalmed in vast lakes against the vast, deep blue skies. Or to fish for trouts in streams of stately forests. It is hard for weekend tourists to notice the real Kashmir. For "elsewhere in the valley of Kashmir, which is ruled by India, the Indian military has been fighting since 1990 a particularly brutal war with thousands of Muslim guerrillas" (Mishra 2000, 36).

For one who has studied British imperialism in Asia, it is tempting to say that the current problems faced by India and Pakistan over Kashmir can be traced to their British legacies, particularly the policy of divide and rule. But the two governments have had more than fifty years to resolve the issue. It is certainly unreasonable to attribute such a complex problem to a single British policy. Indeed Indian and Pakistani scholars have indicated that India had been divided by religion, language, and culture long before British colonization. Religious and ethnic conflicts have dogged Indian rulers for centuries. The British, no doubt, exploited this precolonial conflict for its own ends.

Still the fratricidal wars that took place during and after Partition cannot be completely attributed to the British although many Indian scholars were able to trace their discontent to some policies during the colonial era.[7] Certainly there is no reason to attribute the 1948 and 1965 wars over Kashmir to British colonial policy. But India's neglect of economic development in Kashmir has been a strong contributory factor. Many Indian scholars tended to blame Nehru for not having a vision or development plan for India. But that is not true. He had a plan for India and hoped that its development would spill over to Kashmir. He wanted to accomplish in his lifetime an India that is a self-supporting industrial power. He built vast steel plants in Rourkela and Bhilal, the mammoth Bhakra Dam, the space and nuclear research centers. It even laid out a modern city of Chandigarh built by le Corbusier. "But like the monoliths of Egypt, they towered above the people without altering their lives in a sufficiently rapid and beneficial way" (Desai 1997, 3).

What has long been clear is that the India-Pakistan War over Kashmir has been a compound of so many factors: unresolved historical and territorial issues; war of civilizations (Hindu vs. Muslim), colonial legacy of divide and rule; India's neglect of Kashmir's economic development, secessionist uprisings; the U.S. CIA training and abandonment of Kashmiri youths to fight the Soviet regime in Afghanistan; India's refusal to involve Pakistan or any other country in what it considers to be an internal matter; and Pakistan's support of Kashmir's right of self-determination.

Conclusion

The challenge before the Indian and Pakistani governments is how to come up with a common program to address social and communal problems begotten by that history. These issues were confronted at the outset of independence, through the agony of Partition, and then through military confrontations including two major wars and the building and installation of nuclear weapons. But it has been shown for fifty-five years that they were not the proper solutions to the larger social, political, and economic problems of Kashmir. Despite all the bewildering factors complicating the war over Kashmir, what emerges clearly is that both India and Pakistan want to impose sovereignty over Kashmir. The Indians insist that the maharajah's accession is final while the Pakistanis insist otherwise.

The power of the Indian government is strong over Kashmir, since the accession rested on the forces of violence it commanded over Kashmir. In addition to its Army, India's government has at its disposal powerful secret Police organizations established in the early years of accession. Similarly it would be hardly necessary to repeat that power of Pakistan over many Kashmiris rested on its ability to provide the counterbalancing force in the valley. Moreover, Pakistan has at its command several Islamic jihadi groups that it can send readily to the Kashmir Valley. And according to some analysts, Musharraf's real objective has been to take over Kashmir. In 1999 as Army chief, he sent Pakistani troops to capture the mountainous border territory of Kargil inside the Indian Kashmir (Jones 2002) that led to war with India. It was only defused when then U.S. Pres. Bill Clinton pressured Prime Minister Nawaz Sharif to withdraw his army.

The wars were fought neither to settle unresolved historical issues nor to correct injustices arising from the policy of divide and rule but with a view on both sides to exercise sovereignty or influence over Kashmir. Historical injustice, religious tensions, the Partition, policy of divide and rule, and acts of terrorism have prevented us from seeing clearly this elemental motivation. Yet all lines of inquiry, it seems, lead back to it.

The conflict could be easily resolved if both sides just withdrew their forces of violence and allow the Kashmiri people to decide for themselves whether they want independence or accession to India or Pakistan.

References

Ahmed, Akbar S. 1997. *Jinnah, Pakistan and Islamic identity: The search for Saladin.* Routledge.

Asian Age. 2000. 9 August.

Associated Press. 2002. "India, Pakistan blame each other for crisis." 4 June.

Banga' Indu, ed. 1997. *Five Punjabi centuries: Policy, economy, society, and culture, c. 1500–1990*. New Delhi: Manohar.

Bodansky, Yossef. 2002. *Bin Laden: The man who declared war on America.* Forum.

Burke, S. M. and Quaraishi, Salim Al-Din. 1995. *The British raj in India: An historical review.* Oxford University Press.

De Bellaigue, Christopher. 2001. "The perils of Pakistan." *The New York Review of Books*. 15 November.

Desai, Anita. 1997. "India: The seed of destruction." *The New York Review of Books*. 27 June.

Frank, Katherine. 2001. *Indira: The life of Indira Nehru Ghandi.* London: Harper Collins.

French, Patrick 1997. *Liberty or death: India's journey to independence and division*. Harper-Collins.

Gopal, Sarvepalli. 1980. *Jawaharlal Nehru: A biography.* Vol. 3. Harvard University Press.

Guha, Ramachandra. 1992. *A subaltern studies reader*. University of California Press.

Jha, Prem Shankar. 1996. *Kashmir, 1947: Rival versions of history.* Delhi: Oxford University Press.

Jones, Owen Bennet. 2002. *Pakistan: The eye of the storm*. Yale University Press.

Kashmir Times. 28 June 2000.

Khan, Mohammad Ishaq. 1997. *Experiencing Islam.* New Delhi: Sterling.

MacFarquhar, Roderick. 1997. "India: The imprint of empire." *The New York Review of Books*. 23 October.

McForan, Desmond. 1988. *The world held hostage: The war waged by international terrorism.* St. Martin's.

Mishra, Pankaj. 2000. "The birth of a nation." *The New York Review of Books*. 5 October.

———. 2001. "Murder in India." *The New York Review of Books*. 15 August.

Nehru, Jawaharlal. 1980. *An autobiography.* Oxford University Press.

Pandey, Gyanendra. 1997. "In defense of fragment: Writing about Hindu-Muslim riots in India today." In *A subaltern studies reader, 1986–1995,* ed. Guha Ranajit. University of Minnesota Press.

Powers, Thomas. 2002. "The trouble with CIA." *The New York Review of Books*. 17 January.

Puri, Balraj. 1995. *Kashmir: Towards insurgency.* New Delhi: Orient Longman.

Ramana, M. V. and A. H. Nayyar. 2001. "India, Pakistan and the bomb." *Scientific American* (December).

Rashid, Ahmed. 2002. "Pakistan on the edge." *The New York Review of Books*. 10 October.

Reuters. 2002. "Tension lingers despite summit." 6 January.

Reeve, Simon. 2002. *The new jackals: Ramzi Yousef, Osama bin Laden and the future of terrorism.* Northeastern University Press.

Rubenstein, Richard. 1987. *Alchemists of revolution: Terrorism in the modern world.* Basic Books.

Schofield, Victoria. 2000. *Kashmir in conflict: India, Pakistan, and the unfinished war.* I. B. Taurus.

Sen, Amartya. 1997. "Tagore and India". *The New York Review of Books*. 27 June.

Sengupta, Nitish. 1997. "Partition need not happen if…." *Times of India*. 6 August.

Singh, Karan. 1989. *Autobiography.* Oxford University Press.

Yousaf, Brig. Gen. Mohammad and Maj. Mark Adkin. 1992. *The bear trap.* London: Leo Cooper

Beyond the Bloodshed: Terrorism's Toll on Asian Economies

Cielito F. Habito

More than the loss of thousands of human lives and countless injuries directly resulting from 9/11, those brazen acts of terrorism has had far-reaching repercussions all over the world never before seen arising out of a single incident. Its multidimensional impact on people around the globe span the psychological, social, spiritual, political, and economic facets of human life. The events of September 11 merely epitomized the larger phenomenon of terrorism that has become a seemingly inevitable feature of modern civilization. Asia, being home to over half of the world's population, bears the greater brunt of the adverse consequences of terrorism, whether occurring within or beyond its boundaries.

This essay examines the economic costs of the September 11 attacks on the Asian economies, as an illustration of the impacts of terrorism in general on Asian people's economic lives. That entire economies and individuals' economic welfare have suffered adverse consequences is obvious to anyone living in this part of the world. The paper attempts to identify and document some of these effects in order to gain a fuller appreciation of the economic costs of the September 11 terrorist attack in particular, and acts of terrorism in general. It is hoped that such understanding in turn helps us to muster the wisdom, the will, and the resources to address the problem more definitively.

General Economic Fallout from September 11

The World Bank has projected that the general economic slowdown that affected most countries after September 11 will reduce overall world economic growth by about 1 percent (World Bank 1999). The industries most immediately hit were the airline and insurance industries, with far-reaching effects on other economic sectors.

In the days following the attacks in New York and Washington, U.S. employers cut more than 248,000 jobs, with the transportation sector being especially affected, with more than 96,000 lay-offs (Asia-Pacific Foundation of Canada Website). The attacks also significantly curbed consumer spending, which normally accounts for about two-thirds of U.S. economic activity.

Direct Hit: The Insurance Industry

The losses from the World Trade Center attack were staggering for insurers from many countries. Lloyd's of London anticipated claims amounting to US$1.9 billion. Swiss Re, a major reinsurer (a business that insures regular insurance companies against an unexpected surge in claims) in turn projected US$1.24 billion in claims resulting from the U.S. attacks. Estimates placed the overall cost of insurance claims resulting from the September 11 horrors at about US$35 billion (ibid.).

The logical consequence of these is a dramatic rise in insurance prices, while demand for insurance also grows in anticipation of additional acts of terrorism by Osama bin Laden's al-Qaeda network. These price hikes are passed on to other companies, to governments, and ultimately to the individual taxpayer and consumer.

The cost of traded goods, including food and other basic consumer items, is likely to rise to reflect higher freight insurance costs. Anticipating this, Egypt reportedly made unusually large purchases of U.S. wheat following the attacks. Pakistan faced significant price increases for certain imports, again due to rising freight insurance costs (Hayes 2002).

Higher insurance costs have also affected the cost of air travel. New surcharges to cover increased insurance costs have been imposed by airlines. Thai International Airways added a US$1.25 surcharge to most of its flights on October 1, 2001. Chinese carriers were authorized by the Chinese government to levy surcharges of up to US$2.50 per passenger on international routes. Similarly, Alitalia imposed a "crisis surcharge" of US$5.50 for each leg of an air journey (Asia-Pacific Foundation of Canada Website). Philippine Airlines now charges US$12.00 for "war risk insurance" for international plane tickets.

Major Casualty: The Airline Industry

In the aftermath of the World Trade Center attack, the global civil aviation industry plunged into its worst crisis in more than fifty years, costing the sector an estimated 400 thousand jobs around the world (Hayes 2002). The International Labor Organization reported in January 2002 that the attacks affected every segment in the industry—carriers, airports, aircraft manufacturers, services, parking lots, and vehicle rentals.

Airlines throughout the world have faced heavy losses resulting from higher airline insurance costs and security expenditures, along with a general decline in passenger traffic. The airline industry is a major factor in the overall health of an industrialized economy. In the United States, for example, the industry accounts for 10 percent of the gross domestic product, directly and indirectly.

In Europe, the airline industry was put under great stress. The Belgian carrier Sabena filed for bankruptcy, while government bailouts had to be provided for airlines in France and Switzerland. Major carriers in Britain, Italy, the Netherlands, and Scandinavia cut flight capacity, scrapped certain routes and laid off tens of thousands of employees. Some European airlines added "crisis" or "war" surcharges to their regular ticket prices, to help defray the soaring insurance costs.

In Asia, Malaysian Airlines System cut twelve international flights soon after the September 11 attacks. Korean Air suspended flights on five international routes and reduced four others temporarily, while another Korean airline, Asiana, slashed 1,200 jobs. Japan Airlines and All Nippon Airways also scrapped some international flights (Asia-Pacific Foundation of Canada Website).

Both increased cost of air travel and heightened apprehension about the safety of traveling by air have impacted heavily on tourism. Passenger traffic to and from the United States especially dropped dramatically after the World Trade Center attack. Passenger movements in and out of Europe likewise dropped significantly. These had an adverse impact on tourism-related businesses worldwide, including Asia, being a popular destination for both American and European tourists. Severely affected were hotels, restaurants, resorts and other recreational facilities, retail establishments, and even livelihoods in the informal sector like street vendors.

Asian Economies in the Aftermath of September 11

As the single largest economy in the world, the United States economy is closely linked to most Asian economies through trade, tourism, and/or investments. Among the Southeast Asian countries, the Philippines is the most dependent on the U.S. as an export market, and ranks second to Japan relative to Asia (see table 1).

Table 1. Export Dependence on the U.S., Selected Asian Countries

Percent Share of Exports to U.S. to Total		
COUNTRY	2001	2002
China	24.34	20.92
India	20.88	22.82
Indonesia	15.00	15.54
Japan	31.58	30.05
Korea	20.93	22.48
Malaysia	20.23	20.55
Philippines	26.49	28.67
Thailand	20.34	22.56

Source: Asian Development Bank

Thus, when the U.S. economy practically ground to a halt in the immediate aftermath of 9/11, the repercussions were immediately felt in the economies of Asia and elsewhere in the world. There is much anecdotal evidence to illustrate these impacts:

• China Cargo Airlines, China's largest airfreight shipper, reported that the volume of incoming and outgoing cargo shipped in

November 2001 fell by more than 10 percent compared with a year earlier. That came on top of a similar double-digit drop in October in spite of the fact that it included some backed-up cargo that had been grounded in the days after the September attacks (ibid.).

• After September 11, the tourism industry suffered heavy losses as the number of travelers to China from western countries decreased substantially. According to official estimates, cancelled flights, higher insurance fees, and need for tighter security cost Chinese airlines about 346 million yuan (US$60 million) in lost revenue over a four-month period as a direct result of the terrorist attacks. Both Hong Kong and China suffered serious losses in the hotel industry as a result of reduced travel after September 11. Major hotel chains owned by Hong Kong and mainland citizens reported profit reduction in the range of 60–80 percent in the year to December 31, 2001 (ibid.).

• In Hong Kong, all industry sectors reported lost revenues in 2001, partly due to the recession and partly as impact of the terrorist attacks. The budget deficit ballooned to HK$60 billion (US$10 billion), far above the government's prediction of HK$3 billion. Private sector reaction to Hong Kong's economic slowdown has included a decline in SME and consumer confidence; a shift in focus by the tourist industry away from North America and Europe to mainland China and Taiwan; and substantial job and profit losses at hotels, airlines, and travel agencies (Chino 2001).

• In Japan, tourist travel outside the country declined precipitously, while incoming tourist flows likewise dropped. About 78,000 trips to Okinawa were reportedly cancelled from September 11 to October 10. Japanese airlines suffered, although the impacts on All Nippon Airlines (ANA) have been less severe since ANA is primarily a domestic carrier. Nonetheless both Japan Airlines (JAL) and ANA reduced international capacity, and both have adjusted earlier forecasts and now expect to lose money in fiscal year 2002, rather than show a modest profit as originally projected. Losses reflect slowdowns in cargo revenue as well as declines in the number of passengers (Asia-Pacific Foundation of Canada Website).

• Also in Japan, Taisei Fire and Marine Insurance failed in November 2001, citing liabilities related to the September 11 attacks. The total September 11 bill facing Japanese casualty insurers was (as of late November) estimated to amount to 132.8 billion yen, or just over US$1 billion (ibid.).

• In Indonesia, fear of lack of security drove foreign tourists to cancel trips in 2001, particularly in October and November. The country hosted 5.15 million foreign visitors in 2001, somewhat below the already downward-revised government target of 5.3 million. Before September the official target had been 5.8 million. The resort island of Bali suffered most, with monthly arrivals falling 8.3, 26.5, and 23.6 percent in September, October, and November 2001, respectively (Chino 2001a).

• In South Korea, GNP growth projections for 2002 were slashed in the wake of the terrorist attacks from the 4 percent forecast in July 2001 to 2.2 percent. Subsequent estimates reversed this, putting South Korea's growth rate in 2001 at 2.8 percent and expected to return to around 4.3 percent in 2002 (ibid.).

• Pakistan's economy was directly affected on a variety of fronts, ranging from a severe drop in export orders, to increased expenditure requirements for refugees, to reduced tax revenues, to a sharp slowdown in planned privatization initiatives. By early October 2001, eight foreign carriers had suspended flights into Pakistan, while freight insurance surcharges were driving up the costs of imports to that country. Masood Ali Khan, head of Pakistan's Tourism Development Corporation, predicted a decline in tourism of between 80 and 90 percent for the months following September 2001 (Hayes 2002).

• In Cambodia, which nets about US$120 million a year from tourism, the number of tourists visiting Angkor Wat, Cambodia's major source of foreign exchange, dropped by 40 percent in the months after the September 11 attacks. The government reported that 30 percent of foreign tourists canceled bookings in the second half on All Nippon Airlines (ANA) have been less severe since ANA is primarily a domestic carrier. Nonetheless both Japan Airlines (JAL) and ANA reduced international capacity, and both have adjusted earlier forecasts and now expect to lose money in fiscal year 2002, rather than show a modest profit as originally projected. Losses reflect slowdowns in cargo revenue as well as declines in the number of passengers (Asia-Pacific Foundation of Canada Website).

• Also in Japan, Taisei Fire and Marine Insurance failed in November 2001, citing liabilities related to the September 11 attacks. The total September 11 bill facing Japanese casualty insurers was (as of late November) estimated to amount to 132.8 billion yen, or just over US$1 billion (ibid.).

Table 2. Average Hotel Occupany Rates in Metro Manila by Classification

	Occupancy Rates (Percent)			
Period	DeLuxe	First Class	Standard	Economy
2000	65.3	50.8	53.1	38.0
2001				
January	58.0	49.1	51.0	37.7
February	66.4	62.3	55.6	39.9
March	61.6	64.0	54.8	43.2
April	62.0	61.3	56.2	43.3
May	55.3	55.6	52.1	47.4
June	55.5	51.1	50.1	46.6
July	56.2	50.9	53.6	48.4
August	58.4	55.2	53.3	44.3
September	60.3	57.6	51.7	40.6
October	51.2	49.6	51.3	34.9
November	57.7	53.1	53.6	37.1
December	56.0	47.2	49.9	37.0

Source: Philippine Statistical Yearbook 2002

Exports to the United States also dropped significantly after September 2001. Whereas value of monthly exports to the U.S. had ranged from US$730 million to US$800 million in the earlier part of 2001, this had dropped to just US$702 million by November, and dropped further below US$700 million in the succeeding months (table 3) (ibid.).

Table 3. Total Philippine Exports and Exports to the U.S., June 2001–May 2002

Period	Total Exports (Million US$ FOB)	Exports to U.S. (Million US$ FOB)
2001		768.20
June	2,578.20	775.90
July	2,594.40	728.80
August	2,620.80	790.00
September	2,731.00	799.60
October	2,940.80	701.60
November	2,629.50	702.50
December	2,645.50	
2002		650.40
January	2,631.50	657.40
February	2,627.90	714.20
March	2,849.10	699.60
April	2,748.70	714.30
May	2,917.10	

Source: Asian Development Bank

Economic Rewards for Loyal Allies?

On the other hand, the World Trade Center attack and the subsequent U.S. war on terrorism had apparently also led to some positive payoffs for certain Asian economies, particularly those seen to be supportive of the U.S. campaign. Pakistan's decision to align itself with the U.S. in its attack on Afghanistan drew substantial economic rewards from the superpower, notwithstanding previous sanctions that sought to penalize the country (along with India) for undertaking nuclear tests and maintaining a nuclear arsenal. These sanctions were lifted in October 2001, clearly motivated by the cooperative posture Pakistan adopted on the U.S. war on terrorism.

Meeting Pres. Pervez Musharraf on the sidelines of the UN General Assembly in New York on November 11, Pres. George W. Bush pledged more than US$1 billion in assistance to Pakistan. The funds were to go toward refugee relief and counterterrorism measures, border security, trade and investment support, and debt forgiveness.

Meanwhile, the Asian Development Bank increased its financial assistance to Pakistan from US$626 million to US$950 million. The World Bank gave US$300 million for reform of the banking sector, and in December, the IMF approved a three-year US$1.3 billion loan to Pakistan to combat poverty and adjust to the war on terrorism, with a first installment of US$109 million (Chino 2001).

The Paris Club, comprising of Pakistan's official creditors, restructured US$12.5 billion of Pakistan's external debt, making two-thirds payable over 38 years, and the remainder over 23 years with 15-year and 5-year grace periods respectively. The deal is said to be the equivalent of cutting Pakistan's debt by 30 percent. The deal also made provisions for potential debt-for-aid swaps.

Seemingly on a roll, Pakistan obtained further favors from Europe in October, when the latter agreed to increase its imports from Pakistan by 15 percent up to 2004, while cutting or removing tariffs on selected products from the latter. Moody's Investor Services increased Pakistan's sovereign rating from negative to stable on October 30, based on the support from foreign lenders. And by early 2002, the Karachi Stock Exchange was actually the best performing stock market in the world, with investor confidence seemingly boosted by the massive support spearheaded by the United States.

The Philippines was a similar recipient of U.S. largesse, after coming out in support of the U.S., and even hosting U.S. troops purportedly to "train Philippine soldiers in counterterrorism." With the Abu Sayyaf and the CPP-NPA being prominent in the U.S. list of foreign terrorist organizations, U.S. interest in bringing the war on terrorism to the Philippines was widely expected. Having expressed open support for this war, a visit by Pres. Gloria Macapagal-Arroyo to Washington paved the way for over US$4 billion in military assistance, trade concessions, investment intentions, and veterans' benefits from the U.S. Congress, among others. And as if responding to positive sentiment fuelled by or even influenced by the Americans, the Philippine stock market also perked up in the early part of this year in similar fashion to Pakistan's, although the bullish mood has since dissipated. Interestingly, even as the region's currencies have generally strengthened in the face of a weakened U.S. dollar in recent months, the Philippine peso has remained weak and diverged from its neighboring currencies. No small part of the explanation is the fact that lingering concerns about the threat from remaining terrorist forces at large continue to inhibit confidence in the Philippine economy.

Terrorism in Asia: An Inevitable Fact of Life?

Many Asian countries do not need the World Trade Center attack to feel the brunt of terrorism. The Philippines, Sri Lanka, Pakistan, Indonesia, China, and even Japan are among Asian countries that have had their share of internal terrorist attacks. As with September 11, these acts of terrorism right at home take a toll well beyond the blood spilled and the lives lost in their wake.

Terrorism, whether motivated by insurgency, separatism, rebellion, or plain criminality, exacts a significant toll on people's economic, social, cultural, political, spiritual, and ecological well-being. The lack of peace and security in communities and in society as a whole, and of general political stability, provide an inhospitable environment for economic activities, whether for big business or for small and medium enterprises (SMEs). For markets to function, a key prerequisite is respect for rules and enforcement of contracts. In their absence, economic enterprise and initiative are severely inhibited. Innovation and creativity cannot flourish, and economies tend to operate in a "survival mode."

A casual review of the history of technology, innovation, and enterprise around the globe indicates that the greatest gains in productivity occurred in periods and in places where relative peace and stability prevailed. The United States after the turbulent sixties, Japan through most of the postwar era, and Singapore, Malaysia and Thailand in the eighties and nineties all exemplify this general observation. In contrast, much of Latin America, turbulent through most of the seventies and eighties; Central and Eastern Europe, similarly unsettled for most of the seventies and eighties; much of Africa, marked with deprivation, disparities, and discontent through the past decades; and closer to home, the Philippines and Indonesia, bogged down by social and political unrest since the seventees—all have been marked with sluggish economies and inability to overcome widespread poverty.

Terrorism and socioeconomic turmoil feed on each other in a continuing vicious cycle that needs to be broken if peace, security, and stability are to be attained. But even the most seasoned military strategists would readily concede that breaking the cycle is best attacked on the socioeconomic side. Military solutions alone cannot provide a satisfactory nor sustainable outcome.

Concluding Remarks

During the Johannesburg World Summit on Sustainable Development—where I had the privilege of addressing several audiences on some of the various facets of sustainable development, including environmental protection, financing, and people empowerment through multistakeholder participation in governance—U.S. Sec. of State Colin Powell brought up the topic of terrorism in relation to sustainable development and was met with boos and jeers from the gallery and the hallways of the convention center. While the heckling he received during his speech reflected in part the disagreement over the United States' approach towards international terrorism, I don't believe anyone there disagreed that terrorism and lack of peace indeed represent a formidable obstacle to sustainable development.

As Pres. Gloria Macapagal-Arroyo and many others have rightly asserted, this issue, which is of vital importance to all of humanity, should bring us back to the root cause of it all, and that is *poverty* and *glaring inequities* both among countries and within countries themselves.

Paul Samuelson, in the first chapter of his now classic basic economics text (Samuelson and Nordhaus 2001), highlights the choices any economy must make using two symbolic goods: guns and butter. What he does not explain is that if an economy chooses butter, and ensures that everyone has an equitable share of it, there wouldn't even be any need for guns at all.

References

Asia Pacific Foundation of Canada Website

Chino, Tadao. 2001. "September 11: The Downturn is hitting Asians hard." *International Herald Tribune*. 25 October.

———. 2001a. Opening Remarks at the ADB Institute 4th Anniversary Conference. Tokyo, Japan. 7 December.

Hayes, Harry. 2002. "Economic costs of terrorism." *International Review*. 29 January.

Samuelson, Paul A. and William D. Nordhaus. 2001. *Economics*. 17th ed. Irwin McGraw-Hill.

World Bank. 1999. *Global economic outlook.*